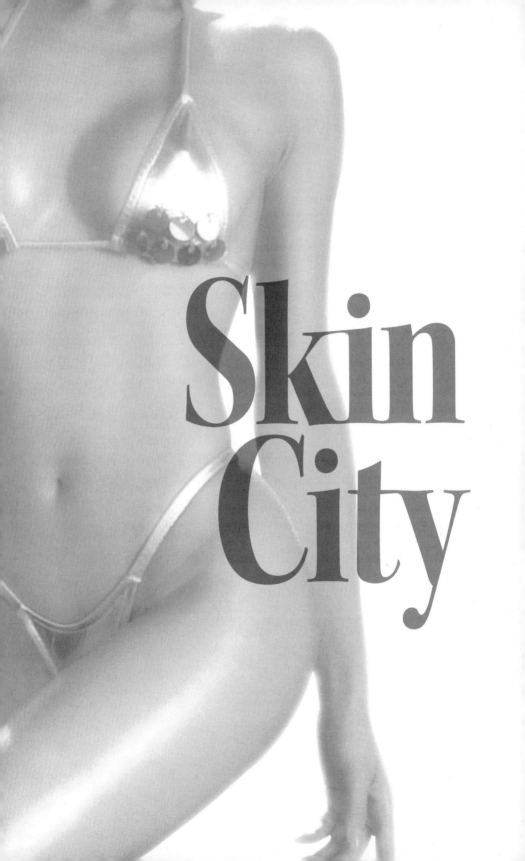

Skin
City

Skin City

Uncovering the Las Vegas Sex Industry

Jack Sheehan

Stephens
Press LLC

A STEPHENS MEDIA GROUP COMPANY

LAS VEGAS, NEVADA

Editor, A. D. Hopkins, Copy Editor, Laura Brundige, Photo Director, Jim Laurie
Photographer, Joseph Pickett III, Bill Hughes, and Las Vegas Stock
Jacket Design, Chris Wheeler, and Sue Campbell, Book Design, Sue Campbell

Sheehan, Jack

Skin city: uncovering the Las Vegas sex industry/Jack Sheehan. –Las Vegas, Nev.:
Stephens Press, 2004.

    p. : cm.

    ISBN: 1-932173-04-8

    1. Sex-oriented businesses—Nevada—Las Vegas. 2. Sex customs—Nevada—
Las Vegas. 3. Prostitution—Nevada—Las Vegas. 4. Las Vegas (Nev.)—Social
life and customs. l. Title.

HQ146.l37 S54 2004

306.74/09793/135—dc22   0405

Stephens Press LLC

A STEPHENS MEDIA GROUP COMPANY

PO Box 1600, Las Vegas, Nevada 89125-1600

702-387-5260 / 702-387-2997 FAX

www.stephenspress.com

Printed in Hong Kong

Dedication

The question I've been asked most often by friends who inquire about this project, other than, "Do you need any help with your research?" is, "How did your wife allow a guy like you to write this book?" The answer, pure and simple, is that she trusts me. And I trust her. And for that and a thousand other reasons, I dedicate this book to Carol Carpenter Sheehan, my wife, lover, best friend, and mother of our two amazing children.

p.s. Carol even talked several of her friends into enrolling in the Strippers 101 class for housewives with her. The class is taught by one of the subjects of this book. Think of the money that might save me!—J.S.

Acknowledgements

I owe gratitude to many people for their help in compiling a book that had many trapdoors. I must thank the over 100 people who agreed to be interviewed, because there were about an equal number who declined. In many cases, the subjects took chances by telling their stories, but they also wanted to set the record straight about their lives in the adult world of Las Vegas. I appreciate their trust, and their time. Thanks to Carolyn Uber of Stephens Press for believing in this project and to Mr. Jack Stephens, a great man in so many ways, for his friendship and stewardship. Thanks also to Craig Campbell of Stephens Inc. for his believing in me. Laura Brundige and A.D. Hopkins did yeoman work in editing the manuscript, and allowing me to indulge myself throughout the process. Both helped make this a better read. Thanks to Sherm Frederick, who invited me into the Stephens Press family, and Max Baer Jr., for being Jethro. Thanks to Bob Stoldal, for allowing me to raid his amazing collection of Nevada history books, and to George Knapp, the best investigative reporter in these parts, for sharing his extensive knowledge of the subject. And to Kim — you know who you are. Thanks also to Sheriff Bill Young, Mayor Oscar Goodman, and Steve Wynn for sharing their valuable time and considerable wisdom. Thanks to John Irsfeld, for his long tenure as my writing mentor. And a special thanks to Christi Lake, who was willing to answer dozens of questions in the last two years on topics that I thought I understood, but didn't have a clue about. Thanks also to the proprietors of Ice, Shari's Ranch Brothel, and Mc Mullen's Pub. And finally, thanks to all the nuns at St. Augustine's Grade School, who told me for eight years that if I thought about sex too much I'd go straight to hell. I can only hope they were wrong.

Contents

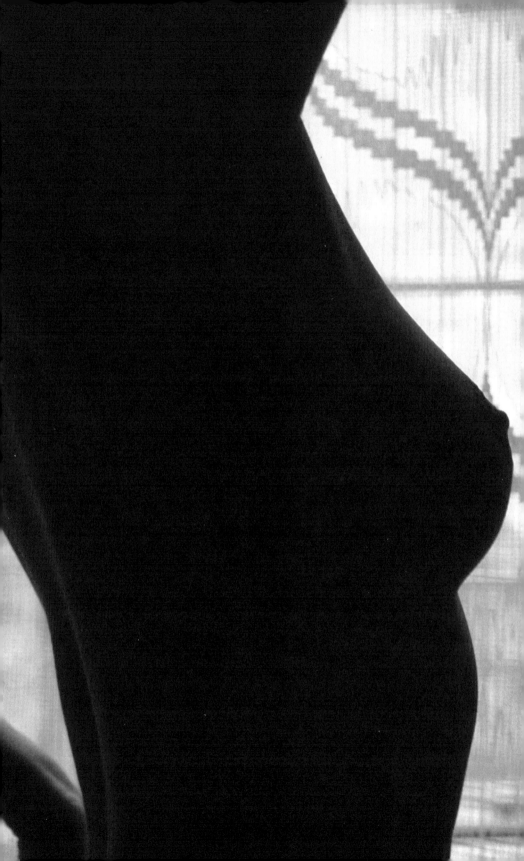

The Scarlet Brick Road to Skin City

The program was full of luscious color pictures of real naked women prancing around on stage in front of an audience. I not only had never seen such a thing; I couldn't imagine that moments such as these could even exist in the cloistered world in which I was raised. I was not yet at the point where the nuns at my school were talking to us about "family matters." The closest I had gotten to sexual awareness was noticing that Pam Connors, the girl in the row next to me, was beginning to stretch the fibers of her school-issued cotton blouses.

My parents had brought the program home to Spokane, Washington after attending a dental convention in Las Vegas. The year was 1960. I was but 11 years old, and when I found the publication in a sack full of goodies and souvenirs, which included a set of plastic false teeth that chattered when placed on a flat surface, I snuck it downstairs and hid it behind a basement bookshelf. It was, I would discover weeks later when I got beyond the pictures to the words, the official souvenir program of *Les Folies Bergere* at the Tropicana Hotel.

The trip south from Spokane had a dual purpose: for my father to attend a one-day dental seminar, and for my parents to watch the Tournament of Champions at the Desert Inn with a group of dentists and their wives. I suppose every family with a working dad has perks that go with his profession. Mine was that I got my cavities filled for free. Also, having a low pain threshold, I could always talk my father into injecting me with more Novocaine, the preferred numbing agent of the day.

I don't know whether abscessed teeth or crooked bicuspids were discussed much on that trip to Vegas. I do know that my parents also brought home a dice clock that hung on our kitchen wall until my mother rightly decided that it didn't represent anything of value to parochial school children like my older sister and myself. Weeks later it was taken down and replaced with a plaque of our Lady of Lourdes.

Having never at that point seen a copy of *Playboy* magazine, and being a full two years short of the onset of puberty, my only exposure to the unfettered female form was pictures of tribal maidens in *National Geographic*. And the breasts of these no-doubt noble creatures, which hung down like tennis ball canisters, didn't exactly accelerate my race towards manhood. But the showgirls of the *Folies* were a different matter entirely. There was one brunette in particular whose picture I studied by the hour. I would learn decades later that her name was Felicia Atkins. She had a stunning face, reminiscent of Elizabeth Taylor or Joan Collins in their primes, with full lips, hypnotic blue eyes, and amazing breasts, large and firm years before cosmetic surgery would make those attributes available to any woman of means.

As luck would have it, I would interview Ms. Atkins for a magazine article some 25 years later, long after her career in the footlights had come to an end. At the time of our meeting, she was a bartender in Las Vegas. I admitted to her in our conversation that she had formed my first indelible image of Sin City, and she politely thanked me. I would learn that I was not alone in my admiration of her attributes. Through the 1960s and 70s Felicia and her bookend partner from the *Folies*, Joyce Grayson, were major celebrities in Las Vegas, and their buxom images were plastered all over magazines and billboards around the world in the days when the Las Vegas showgirl was considered an American icon. Felicia had appeared on the *Ed Sullivan Show*, had dated numerous celebrities including Elvis Presley, had speaking roles in several motion pictures, and even appeared in April 1958, as *Playboy's* Playmate of the Month.

Somewhere in my prepubescent consciousness registered the notion that women who looked like Felicia Atkins were prancing around without clothes for hundreds of people to ogle, and that, when I was old enough, I had better shag my tail from Spokane to Las Vegas and view the real thing for myself. Years later, following the completion of graduate school and a short stint as a newspaper reporter, I determined that writing professionally was my best chance of making a reasonable living. Although my only visit to Las Vegas had been a one-week trip a couple of years prior, I had experienced enough communal energy in that seven-day stay, and met so many interesting characters, that I knew I had to give the city a longer look.

I recall being invited to a dinner party during that first visit. Unlike social gatherings back home, where everyone pretty much dressed alike, had conventional professions, and conducted dinner-table conversation over which there was general agreement and much head-nodding, the Las Vegas group was an eclectic assortment of people with distinctly diverse occupations and backgrounds. There were a lounge singer, a carpenter, a baccarat dealer, a sports bettor, a professional poker player, a woman who owned a singing telegram service, a semi-retired vaudeville performer who had a juggling act with his brothers on the Strip, and, yes, a call girl. The woman didn't admit as much to me, but my host, whom I had known from his previous life as a golf professional in the Pacific Northwest, confirmed it. I spent the evening trying to get her to reveal what she did, but she artfully dodged any direct questions and thus filled my imagination with all sorts of ribald scenarios. I remember one line she delivered after dinner that was unlike anything I'd ever heard from a woman.

The topic of conversation was Kirk Douglas, whom she had recently seen in a movie. She thought the dimple-chinned actor was quite the hunk, but it was the way she expressed it that stayed with me. She said, "If Kirk Douglas walked in this room right now, I'd drop my panties so fast he'd get pneumonia from the breeze." Everyone laughed at the line, but I was the only one shocked by it. Women in Spokane would have said they thought he was handsome. This lady was providing a graphic visual I would treasure for months. It occurred to me at that very moment that although the climate was arid and the soil hard and brittle, there was far more fertile ground to be plowed by a writer in Las Vegas than in the safe and sterile confines of my hometown.

So that partly explains why, at the age of 26, without any real expectation of employment, I packed my meager belongings into a gutless Ford Granada and drove down through Oregon and northern California and across northern Nevada, south to the desert. I arrived here on the Friday of Super Bowl weekend, 1976.

What I envisioned to be a several-month diversion from the real world has turned into a 28-year career scribbling tales about the people and events in this wonderful and crazy town. Say and think what you will about Las Vegas, it just keeps hurtling forward, somewhat oblivious to the judgments that people make about us and our life choices. We had a shade over 400,000 full-time residents when I got here. We're pushing hard towards two million today. The city is still relatively young — just over 60 years have passed since large hotels started to spring up and create the Las Vegas Strip. We will soon celebrate the centennial of the city's incorporation as a railroad hub and stop-off point between Los Angeles and Salt Lake City. During this growth period we've been allowed to shape and reshape our image many times, and the rest of the world has gone right along with it. The one constant, beyond the gambling, the hotels, the building of Hoover Dam, the development of a huge convention business, the shaping of an attractive retirement community and all the rest, is the lure of sex. It was here in 1905 when the town was born, it was magnified when Bugsy Siegel and his contemporaries started building and marketing their luxury palaces, and it's here today. And I'd be less than honest if I didn't admit that my own curiosity about sex and the people who make their living peddling it topped the short list of my reasons for coming here and settling in.

I've written a book on Las Vegas gaming history, another on the unique beauty of the area, and articles about every profession imaginable. And through the years I've penned the occasional article on the people who comprise the "sin" part of Sin City. I've profiled exotic dancers, hookers, gigolos, strip club owners, escorts, and the like. But I had never before now jumped with both feet into the deep water of the adult entertainment scene that draws tens of millions of people here each year.

The seeds for this book were planted two years ago when I wrote a magazine profile on a former student of mine, from my years teaching writing and literature at University of Nevada, Las Vegas.

The article, entitled "B-Student in an X-Rated World" appeared in *Las Vegas Life* magazine, and a revised version is contained in this book as well. Normally I'll hear a few comments about an article in the days and weeks following a magazine's release, but the shelf life of periodicals, and the attention span of those who read them, is short. Books stick around; newspapers and magazines catch next week's parakeet droppings. However, for months after the appearance of that particular piece, I heard comments from dozens of people, usually in a subdued tone and out of the corners of their mouths, that they'd enjoyed this peek into the shadows of a person's life, and they wondered whether I planned on doing more articles like it. I also received phone calls from three students who had been in my English 101 class with the girl, whose screen name is Ashlyn Gere, and they were nearly in disbelief that the sweet and pretty lass, who sat in the row next to them, would make such a bold career leap. It made me wonder whether she would have followed that path had she not been raised in Las Vegas, with its openness towards nudity and sexual expression, and how many other young women's stories would shock the socks off their former classmates if they could be brought into the light.

And thus was formed the idea to explore the lives of the people who comprise what I'm calling *Skin City*.

For nearly 30 years now, I have observed the repeated massaging of our city's image through good times and bad. The ad slogans prepared by R&R Partners, the agency which masterminds and films the image-making commercials for Las Vegas, have run the gamut from "the American Way to Play," to "the Resort Bargain of the World," to "What you Want, When you Want It," to "Freedom from Dullsville." But in the last 30 months, in response to an amalgam of factors working against the economy of our tourism-driven city (the tragedy of 9/11, air-travel restrictions, the widespread legalization of casino and riverboat gambling, international conflicts abroad, weakened economic conditions in Mexico and Japan, and publicity about Las Vegas' becoming America's nuclear waste dump), we have begun selling ourselves to the world with the slogan "What Happens Here, Stays Here."

One ad shows an attractive woman crawling into the back of a limousine, letting her hair down from its neatly tied bun, fondling the leather interior, flirting with the driver, then changing clothes en route to the airport and caressing him as he drops her off. The message couldn't be more clear: Las Vegas is a place where you can totally relax your inhibitions and indulge in behaviors you'd never dreamed of back home in Walla Walla.

"Thousands of hours of research go into these campaigns and these slogans," says R&R vice-president Rob Dondero, who has worked on the Las Vegas Convention and Visitors Authority (LVCVA) campaigns for the last 16 years. "We listen to a lot of focus groups. There is a great deal of care behind these themes. With the 'What Happens Here . . .' campaign, we are letting people fill in their own blanks. Whether it's an older couple that decides it's okay to stay up well beyond their normal bedtime and take an extra pass through the buffet line, or people who want to explore their own personal boundaries a little, we're sending out the message that it's all right in Las Vegas."

In response to criticism from some local business owners who thought the ads were damaging to the city's reputation and to their own business interests, LVCVA President Manny Cortez said, "I think our ads are accomplishing what we wanted them to accomplish, and that is to tongue-in-cheek tell you that Las Vegas is what it is, and if you come here your secret is safe with us. To believe that somebody is not going to relocate to Las Vegas because they saw an ad is ludicrous."

While Dondero concurs that the perception for many baby boomers in the 1990s was that Las Vegas was receptive to their bringing children to town, he's quick to point out that the LVCVA never marketed the city as a family destination. "You never saw us advertise on the Disney Channel, or clearly encourage bringing kids to Las Vegas," he says. "We've always been an adult town, but now we're just a little more aggressive about it."

Las Vegas Mayor Oscar Goodman put it this way in an exclusive interview for this book: "The marketing experts came up with the concept of 'freedom' to describe what our city represents. The idea is that people can leave their cares and woes wherever they came from, so that when they come to Las Vegas they don't have to look over their shoulder, and they can do anything up to the point of illegality, not going over the brink, but right to the edge. Let's not hide behind it. We are an adult playground for adult fun.

"I love it when people say I'm the mayor of America's adult playground," Goodman adds. "I want to see Las Vegas thrive economically, and we must constantly be looking for what attracts people. We need to give people choices so that they'll choose Las Vegas over El Paso. I don't want us to be El Paso with casinos; I want us to be Las Vegas with the glitz and glamour and the neon and the electricity and the excitement and the sensuality. If somebody doesn't come here because they think they can have more fun elsewhere, then shame on us."

Regarding the era when many Americans perceived Las Vegas as a family destination, Goodman says, "It didn't work out. There's still plenty for children to do here, if you want to bring them. But the kids can't generate the kind of revenue that the adults can, and we in the city who rely on the taxes derived from the income want the adults playing and playing hard."

Steve Wynn, the visionary hotel builder, arguably had more to do with shaping the image of modern Las Vegas than did anyone else, with his remodeling of the Golden Nugget and his creation of The Mirage, Treasure Island, and Bellagio. Wynn told me that, while the notion of the LVCVA campaign is correct in making clear that Las Vegas is not for families and the commercial taps into a "cunning" dynamic, more subtlety could have been used.

"My version of that commercial would have been this," Wynn says. "It's a shot of a woman from the waist up. She's sitting at a desk, got a pinstriped suit on, and a shirt and tie, but it's Armani. Her hair is back. She's a blonde like Catherine Deneuve and she's wearing glasses, horn-rimmed. And she says in a distinguished voice, 'Research shows that people of every description, no matter their cultural, ethnic, or economic background, all need to cut loose and explore their wildest fantasies.' Then she leans forward, unclips her hair, shakes it, looks up, pulls down the tie, takes off the glasses and says, 'In Las Vegas, we are the world's greatest experts at *that!*'"

"Right now," Wynn says, "the commercial comes across as saying, 'Here you can do something disgraceful and you won't get caught.' I think these commercials are too obvious. I think we don't have an appreciation for subtlety in Las Vegas, but there's every indication that the public does."

Popular new Clark County Sheriff Bill Young told me he views the marketing campaign this way:

"Saying that what goes on here stays here does not necessarily equate to crimes being committed," he said. "It may mean 'Yeah, the guys and I were out in Las Vegas and we went to a topless bar.' Or 'We went out and had a few drinks, or we were looking at some good-looking girls when we were not with our wives.' Or even, 'We partied a lot and got naked and jumped in the Jacuzzi in the hotel room as couples.' But none of that behavior is against the law. I'm certainly not in a position to endorse any activity that would break the law, and the hotels aren't doing that either. But we do want people to come out here and have a great time, and yeah, the message is that we are a little risqué in Las Vegas."

The Sheriff added that when he goes to other cities he enjoys their beauty and uniqueness, but he says, "I get a little bored sometimes at nine or ten o'clock at night when the streets are rolled up. There is no place like Las Vegas."

It's apparent that the powers that be concur that the best way to position Las Vegas in these challenging times — the way to completely distinguish the city from all the other gaming and entertainment venues vying for tourism and convention dollars — is to sell SEX, and to sell it in capital letters.

There's certainly no hiding from it. Sex is everywhere you look along and near the Las Vegas Strip, from the hotel nightclubs, to the more-revealing-than-ever-before shows playing up and down the Boulevard, to the 40 and counting gentlemen's clubs clustered within a short cab ride of the major hotels, to the billboards offering barely clothed beauties "Direct to your Room," to the attractive and well-dressed young women seated patiently in the lobbies and lounges of our finest hotels, pretending to be waiting for husbands. Las Vegas in 2004 is a place determined to get a body's blood boiling at the very thought of coming here.

This is a far cry from just 10 years ago. The January 10, 1994 issue of *TIME* magazine carried a cover story titled, "Las Vegas: The New All-American City." The lengthy report inside, which mixed pictures of various Strip attractions with a half-page photo of a t-shirted young father in a baseball cap carrying an infant through a casino in a backpack, had two sentences near the lead that seem nearly unimaginable a decade later: (1) "The general Las Vegas marketing spin today is that the city is fun for the whole family"; and (2) "...the streets are hookerless and the best-known Vegas strip club, the Palomino, lies discreetly beyond the city limits."

One could only imagine if *TIME* were to revisit us today. The reporter would write something like: (1) Las Vegas is the last place in the country you'd want to bring children, unless they are immune to nude billboards, taxicab signs, and entertainment dripping with sex appeal; and (2) While there's little blatant evidence of hookers on the streets of Las Vegas, they are abundant in even the most luxurious hotels; and those visitors weary of gambling have more strip clubs than Strip hotels to choose from, just a five-dollar cab ride away.

Introduction

One entrepreneurial huckster named Michael Burdick felt that Las Vegas had gone so far down the road of "anything goes" that in the summer of 2003 he started promoting a business he called "Hunting for Bambi." He explained to a local television reporter (with explicit footage included), that men were paying him between $5,000 and $10,000 to hunt down naked women in the desert and shoot them with paintball guns. One of the prey, a woman interviewed in her birthday suit at one of the "hunts," said she was willing to do it because she was being paid $1,000, with an additional bonus of $1,500 if she could elude being hit and captured. Apparently, the national media was so receptive to the licentiousness of Las Vegas that four or five national cable news shows, including Keith Olberman's *Countdown* and CNN's *Newsnight*, hosted by Anderson Cooper, invited Burdick to explain to a national audience why his business was a good idea. Predictably, talking-head defenders of women's rights expressed outrage, and Las Vegas was generally decried as the world capital of sexism and the ninth ring of Dante's Inferno, at least until Burdick confessed days later that the whole story was a hoax designed to market and sell videotapes.

Coincidentally, the day after the Bambi story broke, I was interviewing an exotic dancer and she said dozens of the girls at her club were wondering how to get involved in the business, "because $1,000 to $2,500 for a couple hours in the desert is darned good money."

Through the years, the media and the publishing industry have been unpaid shills for the enticements of Las Vegas, constantly sending out the message that Vegas is the hottest place on the planet for sexy, available women. How many other cities have had two different series named after them? There was the Aaron Spelling production *Vega$*, in the late 70s and early 80s, that reeked of fast cars and fast women and a moral code that offered the private detective Dan Tanna license to sleep with half his clients. This season's NBC series *Las Vegas*, starring James Caan and a supporting cast of hotties, offers more of the same. The premiere episode in September 2003, which scored lofty Nielsen ratings, showed the boss's daughter having sex with his right-hand man; another couple getting it on in a hotel elevator, fully aware that the surveillance cameras were focused on them; and a patron of a gentlemen's club slipping a one hundred-dollar bill into a dancer's g-string — with his teeth. As local puritans shook their heads at what they certainly viewed as another denigration of our city's image, casino owners in unison thought "Cha-Ching!"

And you can't channel surf in the higher numbers, through the Travel Channel and the Discovery Channel and others, without finding a feature on Las Vegas, its showgirls, or its *Real World* temporary occupants in the Palms Hotel shedding their clothes and inhibitions.

A sampling of old books and magazines about Las Vegas dating back to the 1950s, with their lurid prose and pages upon pages of semi-clothed or nude "showgirls," reads like a modern-day version of *Vegas Confidential*.

In an article by Hoyt McAfee in *Sir! A Magazine for Males*, dated December, 1955, we learn that, "As might be expected, the FBI keeps an alert and carefully trained eye on Las Vegas at all times ... . It watches every move of the White Slavers and violators of the Mann Act, and cracks down upon them when they try to set up shop in the Las Vegas area. And so all the 'pleasure dispensers' in Las Vegas today — the molls of the mobsters, the hotel hustlers, the cocktail lounge tarts, the chorus girls who latch on to 'spare change' after working hours, and the stranded girls who decide to turn a fast dollar the lustful way — watch their step and use tact in selling their favors."

The implication is that nearly every woman who works on the Strip is willing to sell her body for the right price.

In *PIC* magazine, also from 1955, Joan Collins is featured on the cover (she was 22 then), and a bannered story by Associated Press reporter Bob Considine titled "Las Vegas Exposed: A Complete Story of Vice" purports to detail the corruption and decadence of the city in the first decade of the Strip's emergence. Beyond Considine's report, the publication is little more than cheesecake shots of showgirls, and sports and war stories suited for "real men."

Crime magazines like *Detective Cases* also took a disparaging look at the city, but in every case the publication uses buxom crime victims or damsels in distress to sell the story. Here's a snippet from a May 1961 issue: "Las Vegas bills itself as the 'Fun and Entertainment Capital of the World.' Well-heeled civic boosters point with moist-eyed pride to the town's rocketing prosperity, its low (recorded) rate of vice and crime. But statistics can be interpreted in various ways, and there is plenty to back up the cry of vice crusaders, both local and national, that the real claim to fame of the glittering Western spa is its role as a major focus of America's creeping moral cancer."

It's no secret that the Las Vegas datelines, especially accompanied by the word "sex," are surefire ways to increase magazine sales and television ratings. It was that way in the 1950s, and it's even more so thus far in the new millennium.

There are estimates that over 15,000 women have received sheriff's cards permitting them to dance either topless or totally nude in Las Vegas strip joints, which are no longer saloons with sawdust on the floor, but upscale art deco emporiums costing upwards of $50 million. I spoke with several dancers about their decision to move to Las Vegas; they were open about the money they were making, the advantages and disadvantages of their career choices, and what really goes on in those VIP rooms that so many hopeful visitors are willing to pay $500 an hour to enter.

You can throw out the stereotype of the stripper as a bubble-headed blonde taking the easy route to a quick buck in support of a drug habit. Oh, there are a few of those. And there are probably too many who are the chief breadwinner behind a lazy boyfriend. But also employed in these clubs are many well-educated and well-bred women who tried the corporate world, got tired of bumping their heads against that glass ceiling, and decided to take their natural beauty (albeit with a few cosmetic enhancements thrown in) and knock down the big bucks for five or six years. An attractive and clearly focused exotic dancer in Las Vegas will make anywhere from $200,000 to $350,000 a year, not all of it reported to Uncle

Introduction

Sam. With good advice from money managers (and there are no shortage of those visiting her place of business) she can be financially set by the age of 35. The allure of nice clothes and private schools for her children can go a long way toward rationalizing a career swinging around a pole and whispering sweet nothings in a stranger's ear. And hey, dancing is good for the heart and lungs as well (as long as too much smoke isn't inhaled).

According to Bianca Paris, a northern California woman who sold three hair salons in tiny Susanville to pursue a career as an exotic dancer, "Las Vegas is the stripping capital of the world. There are more girls making good money here than anyplace else because the business is active from early in the afternoon until ten the next morning. It's absolutely amazing how much money walks into these clubs every night, and how much of it the girls manage to take home."

When I inquired whether security was ever a concern for a petite blonde like herself, Bianca said, "I feel completely safe in the club. The only ones who aren't safe are the men and their wallets."

A little quick math indicates just how important strip clubs are in the overall economy of Las Vegas. A place like Jaguars, where Bianca works, employs well over 500 dancers on a given day. It is one of the larger clubs of the 40 in Clark County. If we estimate that the average number of dancers working at a club is 100, and those girls average $350 a day in tips, then $1.4 million in hard cold cash is slipped into g-strings in a single day. That equates to $430 million a year that's pumped — or shall we say bumped — into our economy. And if my sources are remotely accurate, about 60 percent of these women spend nearly every dime they make.

Dancer Sabrina Markey, who teaches money management to professional dancers as part of her Strippers 101 curriculum, says, "Exotic dancers kept many Las Vegas retail stores afloat following the recession brought on by 9/11. If there's one thing these girls do better than dance, it's shop."

And then there are the young women who have chosen to ply the world's oldest profession. They too were lured to Las Vegas because of its well-earned reputation as a land of milk and honey for adult entertainment. I was able to find one woman, Karin, who had spent her career in various aspects of the adult business, and now functions as a madam to women who command $1,000 an hour. A divorced mother of two young boys, Karin reflected on her 20-year journey through Los Angeles "social clubs" and strip joints to her present position as owner-operator of her own "referral" business. She arranges liaisons, as she puts it, "with only the best-looking, classiest women with the hottest bodies, for an elite clientele of businessmen willing to pay top dollar for just about anything their little libidos desire." As she reflected on her life and the circumstances that brought her to Las Vegas, Karin, said, "Who has a better life than me? I'm making more money than I ever dreamed possible and am able to spend all the quality hours I want with my sons. God Bless America."

Among her 15 regular girls, Karin found two willing to talk with me about the career they've chosen, how the business works for them, and where they see their lives going from here.

Las Vegas has also become home to several adult film stars. Some of them, like my former student, grew up here; others live here because of tax advantages and the proximity to Los Angeles. Our city annually hosts the biggest adult video convention of the year (in conjunction with the Consumer Electronics Show), and the *Adult Video News* Awards which have been called the Porn Oscars. Somehow, I managed to get a ticket and front-row seat at an awards show unlike any you've ever seen. If my mother were looking down that night from heaven and saw her only son at a sex film awards show and a sign on the table identifying him as "Talent," . . . well, Mom . . . forgive me. I'm just trying to scrape out a living here.

And there's even a large and active group of people in Las Vegas who happily share their mates with other free-spirited couples. These swingers, as they are commonly called, range from adult film stars flexing their muscles and other body parts after hours, to couples just looking for open conversation with like-minded adults.

Hank Armstrong and his wife Anna Malle, an adult film star and feature dancer who travels the country, are among the most active swinging couples I met. Anna loves having sex with both men and women, and says she is at times insatiable, while Hank has been known to go through 30 condoms in a day at one of the annual swingers' conventions. But couples like Steve and Allison, who attended the Lifestyles annual swingers' convention at the Aladdin Hotel last August, are more typical swingers. They might hook up with one or two other couples during a four-day convention, but they value the friendships they've made and the camaraderie of the meetings as much as they do the sex.

I also spoke with an enterprising couple, David and Virginia Cooper, who have turned their swinging lifestyle into a business, with one overriding restriction for couples who pay to attend parties at their beautiful ranch-style home: they must be attractive.

In the two years I spent doing research for *Skin City*, I discovered that everyone in the adult business or lifestyle, no matter the degree to which they were willing to take their sexual expression, has his or her own clearly defined personal boundaries. For instance, the madam and call girls I spoke with would not make adult films. They considered it far too exhibitionistic for their tastes. The adult film stars by and large did not consider prostitution an option, nor would they concede for a second that by having sex for money on camera with a relative stranger were they engaging in a form of prostitution. They believe they are exercising their mode of creative expression and providing an outlet for couples to learn more about sexual techniques and add some spice to their lovemaking. And several of the strippers thought it sad that some of their sister dancers occasionally perform sex acts for money. The consensus of opinion was that girls who crossed the line did so either because their cultural background was especially permissive, or they were financially desperate.

One thing is certain: the sex industry in Las Vegas thrives because there are thousands of cooperative people in the service industry — limo drivers, cabbies, valet parkers, bellmen, cocktail waitresses, bartenders, and on and on — who are the first point of contact for visitors with lots of discretionary income stuffed in their pockets and will point those visitors toward whatever adult entertainment they are seeking.

A limo driver named William says the income for drivers ranges from about $35,000 a year for those who play it straight, to more than $100,000 for drivers who will refer call girls, deliver customers to sex/swing clubs, and even sell drugs out of their cars.

"If I get 20 rides a night, I'd say a dozen will ask me where they can get some powder (cocaine) or some Ecstasy," William says. "And maybe another five will want to know where they can get some girls. People who come to Las Vegas by and large want to go absolutely batshit from the time they get here until they leave.

"The city gets by on people scratching one another's backs," he says. "You turn a guy onto a girl whose number is in your cell phone, and she kicks you back 20 percent on the transaction. What's wrong with that? It's the American Way."

I wonder if William knows that the Las Vegas marketing geniuses have already used up that slogan.

The Oscars of Porn

"There is no greater nor keener pleasure than that of bodily love … and none which is more irrational."

— Plato

The air of mock-suspense was palpable. The ballroom on the second floor of the Venetian Hotel, holding 3500 gaudily but scantily dressed revelers, was hushed as the nominees were being read for one of the major awards of an evening that's come to be called "The Oscars of Porn."

Among the contenders for Best Anal Sex Scene in a Video were: Buttfaced! 3, White Trash Whore No. 24, and Hot Bods and Tail Pipe No. 21. And the winner was … Actually, I never heard the name of the winner because by the time the other 12 nominees for the same award were announced, the garbled pronunciations of the presenters had long since been drowned out by private conversations in other parts of the massive room.

I couldn't help thinking that in order to produce sequels to the titles that were being honored this night, there must have been a sizable audience somewhere on the planet willing to buy 23 previous editions of White Trash Whore and 20 episodes of Hot Bods and Tail Pipe.

As easy as it is to poke fun at the *Adult Video News* Awards that are given out each January in Las Vegas, and the outrageous categories that have been concocted to honor nearly everyone who had sex on camera in the last 12 months, the event is indisputably the industry's biggest annual party and the best marketing opportunity for a porn production company to increase video sales and rentals.

There are so many still- and video cameras in the Venetian this night, and such a crush of fans lined up along "the gauntlet" leading to the ballroom of this beautiful hotel (which was constructed, ironically, to recreate the most romantic city in the world) that at first glimpse one might think this ceremony had all the elegance and distinction of the real Academy Awards. At least until two busty blonde women wrap their arms around each other, embrace in a ferocious French kiss, and then release their breasts from their gowns and start to maul each other for the cameras. The explosion of camera strobelights is suddenly blinding. This is what the fans have come to see, and the resulting pictures capturing this tender moment will be used in thousands of international publications over the next several months to celebrate an underground industry which — at least on this night — surfaces for the mainstream to observe and ogle.

I'm attending the festivities with Christi Lake, an adult star who's been a most cooperative and jovial interview for this book, and who has volunteered to serve as my guide for this trek through the jungle. She's even managed to finagle me a ticket with a face value of $225. (Later on I do the math, and discover that if 3000 of the 3500 attendees paid for their tickets, the live gate generated $675,000!)

Christi is wearing a beautiful beaded evening gown which would be appropriate for a lavish charity ball or night at the symphony. Just ahead of us in the procession along the gauntlet are Kathy Willetts and her husband Jeff. They are the couple infamous for his videotaping her having sex with prominent clients in Florida in the mid-1990s. A former police officer, Jeff was eventually charged with pandering and served several months in prison. More than one elected official, including Doug Danzinger, the vice-mayor of Fort Lauderdale, was implicated in the scandal and forced to resign. And the Willetts' defense attorney, Ellis Rubin, pled the infamous "nymphomaniac defense" in explaining that Kathy's behavior with her clients was due to her uncontrollable urge to have sex several times a day. The tabloids ate up the story, and Kathy and Jeff appeared on *Entertainment Tonight*, *Inside Edition*, and *A Current Affair*, as well as in mainstream publications that couldn't resist the tale of sex, political corruption, and the outrageously creative excuse for it all.

The Willetts now live in Las Vegas and produce their own adult videos. This night Kathy is wearing a black mini-dress, which I notice under the bright lights is totally transparent. When the procession stops for more photo ops, Kathy snuggles with an actress named Raquel Divine, who is co-starring with her in a new video, while Jeff stands quietly to the side. I introduce myself to Jeff and compliment his wife on her dress. "It's totally see through," he says, with an approving smile.

"So I notice," I say. I then wonder whether, the arena being what it is, I shouldn't have said something like, "Nice tits," or even, "Your wife has an amazing ass." I sense he would have reacted pretty much the same and thanked me for the kind words.

Jeff and I then chat briefly about our golf games. He complains that he has always had trouble with a killer slice. It occurs to me we could just as easily be two guys shooting the breeze at a Rotary meeting.

Also nearby is Porsche Lynn, a veteran porn star who just recently did a lesbian scene with Christi which is currently in play on Christi's pay-subscriber website. Porsche is dressed in a long black, faux-fur trimmed coat and Russian hat. I tell her she looks like Julie Christie in *Doctor Zhivago*. "Oh, that's my favorite movie," she says. "I've watched it about 20 times, mainly for the fashions."

I learn later from an odd-facts Internet search that Porsche has something in common with a much younger Angie Dickinson. Do you think the average *Jeopardy* contestant could come up with the question to this answer?: These two film actresses are the only ones ever to take out million-dollar insurance policies on their legs.

Chapter 1

Right behind Porsche is Juli Ashton, another legend of the industry who in addition to her adult work has appeared in several softcore movies. She had a sizable role in the film *Orgazmo*, produced by *South Park* creators Trey Parker and Matt Stone, has appeared in a number of films that play late at night on Showtime and other cable channels, and has been the host of the Playboy Network's *Night Calls* television program. Juli's job on *Night Calls* was to interview other porn stars, demonstrate sex toys, and field phone calls from viewers who share their most lurid fantasies. The callers are often engaging in sex while they're making the call, and Juli will prod them toward the finish line. She is an enthusiastic proponent of anal sex and often says things like "If you aren't doing it in the butt, you're missing out on the best part of sex."

Juli is dressed conservatively this evening in a pretty blue pantsuit, and without prior knowledge you'd be hard pressed to believe that a main source of this woman's income is derived through the sale of rubber-and-acetylene molds of her vagina and anus for consumer use. I half expect a devoted fan to hand her a pliable sphincter to autograph.

About every 20 feet or so Christi is stopped for either a print or on-camera interview. And fans continually call out her name. "Christi, we love you!" or "Great dress, Christi, show us your tits."

I'm half-expecting someone to yell out, "Who's that old coot you're with?" but when that doesn't happen I realize the men at these events are merely arm candy to show off the women.

A television interviewer named ChiChi LaRue — a female impersonator and porn producer who resembles the actor Divine from the John Waters classics *Pink Flamingos* and *Hairspray* — fawns over Christi, telling her over and over how stunning she looks.

When I'm introduced to ChiChi, I struggle to make idle conversation. I finally blurt out something about the only other Chi Chi I know being the professional golfer with the last name of Rodriguez, who plays on the Senior PGA Tour. Mr./Ms. LaRue looks at me like I've lost my mind.

Once inside the room, we are seated about 10 rows back from the stage at a table bearing a placard that reads "Talent." Several people walking by our table, fans of the industry who have purchased tickets, give me a funny look. I wonder if they're thinking that I'm some over-the-hill swordsman clinging to my glory days as a porn star. On the table in front of each place setting is a bottle of I.D. Lube, with a card proclaiming that it is the "Official Lubricant of the 2003 AVN Awards Show." It occurs to me that this is surely the only fancy gathering I will ever attend where the table gift is meant to be applied directly to my penis. I also find myself wondering how many other lubricants were in the running before they were beat out by I.D. to have the distinction of being "The Official" lubricant. And how much field-testing was done to determine the eventual winner?

> *. . . this is surely the only fancy gathering I will ever attend where the table gift is meant to be applied directly to my penis.*

Then Christi tugs my arms and says, "Oh, you have to meet Dave. Now there's a story for you." She introduces me to a bald gentleman, in his 60s, with a paunch. He looks like the actor who played Uncle Festus on the *Addams Family* TV show. The man smiles and gives me a firm handshake. "Dave Cummings," he says. "I'm the oldest working actor in adult films."

I assume he's kidding, or that he's a character actor who fills in with a little dialogue between the sex scenes, but that is not the case. He hands me his business card, which reads, Adult Video: Dave Cummings: Actor/Producer/Director. I learn over the next few minutes that Dave was a career Army man, and a former lecturer at West Point. He is 63 years old and has made over 300 adult films.

"I've been filmed getting blowjobs on five different occasions just this week during the convention," he says. I nod and acknowledge that he's five up on me in that department.

"And you need to check out my series, *Kneepad Nymphos*," he says. "We just finished edition no. 6. We're up for several awards tonight."

"And I thought Gene Hackman was the hardest working actor in show business," I say. Dave politely smiles.

Christi is listening in, and she interjects, "Dave and I have a lot in common. We're both very professional and dedicated to this industry. We take our work seriously and treat it like a business. I like Dave very much and I hope I can work with him someday."

> *"I've been filmed getting blowjobs on five different occasions just this week during the convention."*
>
> —DAVE CUMMINGS

Dave's eyebrows catapult at her comment and he gives me a wink. "I'd like that very much," he says.

I learn that Dave got into the business eight years ago, when his girlfriend left him, as he puts it, "for a guy with hair."

"I started to go to Lifestyles conventions for swingers as a way to meet women," he says, "and at one of these I was interviewed by the Playboy Channel."

That appearance got Dave a small part in an adult film, and he was able to perform on cue.

I recall Christi's telling me earlier that a lot of men who would like to be studs in adult films can't get the job done because they are too self-conscious to perform on camera, what with the hot lights, other males holding cameras and microphones close to the action, and the pressure of knowing that if they aren't able to maintain an erection and have an orgasm on camera the film will be a bust. That was not a problem for Dave.

"I was pretty much hooked on it from that first shoot," he says. "I now make all my own films. I write 'em, film 'em (he mimes holding a camera on his right shoulder and pointing down between his legs), and act in 'em."

Dave then tells me that he runs every day, "to keep the legs and other things hard."

I can't help but be intrigued by this man who looks like the guy who sprays for bugs in our back yard, who served our country for 20 years in the military and later taught the best and the brightest at the academy that trained Dwight Eisenhower and Douglas McArthur. And he's more than willing to share his story with me because getting publicity will further advance his film career, his website, and his unique standing among other men his age. Surely he's the only man over 60 years old who's managed to make a living by staying erect on camera, and on cue.

"So how do you do it?" I ask. "Is Viagra the answer?"

"That's what everyone thinks," he says. "Actually, I just love sex and it's not difficult for a guy like me to get excited about pretty young women."

I ask him if he ever speaks to groups of senior citizens, inspiring them to keep a little coal in the old furnace.

"I've spoken to dozens of gatherings," he says. "And it's a lot of fun. I usually get approving looks from the men, who have a lot of questions, but not-so-pleasant looks from the women. I can tell they are thinking, 'Who does this old goat think he is, anyway?'"

Dave tells me he has two grown children, a daughter and a son, and four grandchildren. Both his son and daughter know what he does for a living, but while his son kids him about it around other men, and brags to his cronies about his father the sex-machine, his daughter doesn't like to talk about it.

Just then a flashy blonde, with silicone breasts the size of volleyballs and wearing a dog collar and long crucifix earrings, grabs Dave and gives him a big hug. "Hey, you old stud," she says.

Dave excuses himself and tells me to call him any time. "And don't forget to check out my website," he says. "Dave Cummings dot com."

The opening act for the evening's festivities is Motley Crue lead singer Vince Neill, who belts out a rock number as a dozen partially or totally naked dancers and porn actresses slither across the stage, grooving to the beat. Vince lives in Las Vegas and, true to his profession and to other members of his band, makes no secret of his infatuation with sex and large-breasted women. The confiscated video that showed Neill having sex with porn star Janine and one of her actress friends was the second-best-selling underground sex tape a few years back. Only Motley Crue's drummer Tommy Lee and Pamela Anderson getting cozy in their notorious honeymoon tape shot at

Lake Mead topped it in Internet hits and sales. Who can ever forget the scrawny Lee steering the rented houseboat with his "drumstick?" His band only wishes their most recent music album sold nearly as well as the home movie.

While more mainstream entertainers might find their careers seriously damaged by such erotic romps on tape — think Rob Lowe in Atlanta in the late 1980s — rock stars' bad-boy reputations are only enhanced by the exposure. And when Vince adjourns to a front-row seat after his song, he is mobbed by starlets hugging and kissing him and performing other maneuvers that Dick Clark would surely not approve of were this the American Music Awards.

. . . the category of Male Performer of the Year. There's Erik Everhard, Brandon Iron, Wesley Pipes, Lexington Steele, and Brian Surewood.

When we get to the category of Male Performer of the Year, I can't help but laugh at the names of the finalists. There's Erik Everhard, Brandon Iron, Wesley Pipes, Lexington Steele, and Brian Surewood. I wonder if there's a PR firm in North L.A. that helps sturdy young actors come up with their monikers. I'm about to read them out loud at our table, but I stop myself when I realize that one of these swordsmen might be seated with us. And then I think of two of the more famous names in porn stud history: Harry Reems was the "Deep" of the classic *Deep Throat*, which made a household name of Linda Lovelace (the "Throat"), and provided the alias of the person who provided important information to Woodward and Bernstein and led to the demise of the Nixon Presidency after Watergate. And the aptly named Peter North became legendary in the industry for his ability to generate voluminous amounts of semen and launch it nearly across the room at the climactic moment. North's real name is Al Brown, and his nickname prior to porn stardom was "Beercan" because his discharges resembled someone popping the top on a warm beer after vigorously shaking the can.

"Michael Jackson can call himself whatever he wants," says Christi when the subject of porn studs comes up. "But the real King of 'Pop' was Peter North. You had to be careful on a facial cumshot that you didn't lose an eye."

According to a friend of mine who pays close attention to such things, North had one scene where he actually achieved seven separate ejaculations. "Any single one of them would make a man on his honeymoon proud," he told me. "And I swear there wasn't any editing. The camera never moved."

"Sort of the Barry Bonds of porn?" I suggested.

> *"Any single one of them would make a man on his honeymoon proud."*

"Yeah, but Barry can hit only one at a time," my friend said. "If the guy could bottle his secret, he'd be a millionaire."

I elect not to have him elaborate on his mixed metaphor.

Another highlight of the evening, which draws a partial standing ovation from those paying attention to the activity on stage, is the introduction of *Hustler* magazine publisher Larry Flynt, who is rolled to the podium in his gold-plated wheelchair. Flynt, of course, has spent his life fighting for First Amendment rights and battling censorship, and was the subject of the highly acclaimed 1996 film *The People Vs. Larry Flynt,* which starred Woody Harrelson, Edward Norton, and Courtney Love. He also was involved in a celebrated lawsuit with Reverend Jerry Falwell after *Hustler* named the right-wing preacher their "Asshole of the Month" and satirically accused him of having sex with his mother in an outhouse. In 1988 Flynt won a landmark Supreme Court decision in that case which overturned an earlier ruling in Falwell's favor.

Flynt is at the AVN Awards this evening to present the Reuben Sturman Special Achievement Award, named after a man who lost a celebrated court battle in Las Vegas over the interstate distribution and sale of sex tapes that depicted, among other things, people having sex with animals. The government convicted Sturman on most of the 40 charges that were brought against him, and he died in prison in 1997. Las Vegans may remember Sturman arriving at the Clark County Courthouse each day wearing a white surgical mask and cowboy hat, and how jurors got physically ill watching some of the tapes that prosecutors put into evidence. But on this night, Sturman is lionized by Flynt as a true hero of the industry.

"Reuben paved the way for all of us," Flynt says. "Although he died in prison, he lived a great life and I loved and respected him. He treated his employees as well as the president of any Fortune 400 company."

Flynt is a past winner of the Sturman Award, as are former porn queen Sharon Mitchell, who founded AIM, the Adult Industry Medical company that provides AIDS testing for performers in the business, and Gloria Leonard, former publisher of *High Society* magazine, who is a past president of the Free Speech Coalition. Leonard is probably the only magazine publisher in history whose cover story regularly featured her having sex with other adult-film notables, including the porn legend John Holmes (*more on him in a moment*).

The honoree this night is Mel Kamins, the retired president of General Video Cleveland. Kamins learned the adult film distribution business from Reuben Sturman and his speech is in large part a tribute to his mentor. A grandfatherly man in his 70s, Kamin's remarks are so generic and non-specific to his industry that if you walked in on the middle of his speech you might think he was a distributor of laundry detergent or Post-it notes. He thanks his employees, who have taken out a two-page congratulatory ad in the evening's program, for their loyalty, and says his success has been all about helping others fight their battles. He wishes his daughter, to whom he is leaving the business, good luck in her career.

About midway through the proceedings, I exit to take a bathroom break, and find that there are still thousands of people outside the entrance, taking advantage of spontaneous opportunities to photograph and get signatures from their favorite stars. One notorious producer, Max Hardcore — who recently has spent several days fighting an obscenity battle in a Los Angelescourtroom based on actors in his films portraying characters under the age of 18 — is showing off a young starlet. Eager fans cheer wildly as she flashes her breasts and then jumps up on a counter, spreads her legs, and gives them a "money shot" that they'll surely treasure when they return to Omaha or Tokyo or Amsterdam and get their film developed.

Christi mentions to me that Max Hardcore is one of a contingent of older directors who are really pushing the envelope of kinkiness with their recent videos. This includes more bathroom scenes, and, she says, "Some that show women pissing a lot, but not on each other.

These are directors who have made so many videos that they are bored with conventional stuff. And sadly," she adds, "a lot of the sicker stuff is priced higher."

I notice that the foreign contingent this night is large, and I am told by Christi that hundreds of people annually fly into Las Vegas from all over the globe just for this evening. This annual event for pornophiles is their Oscars, World Cup, and Superbowl rolled into one. And most of them don't have tickets to the show, only cameras to capture spontaneous moments like this.

The 'Adults-Only' Convention

The previous day, I had attended with an actor friend the Adult Entertainment Expo (AEE) at the Sands Convention Center. This exhibitors' show, which was launched in 2000, is an extension of the adult branch of the Consumer Electronics Show (CES), that was started and owned by Venetian Hotel magnate Sheldon Adelson. The adult show has been coming to Las Vegas since the early 1980s, always as an adjunct to the CES convention, but in its first years it was usually cordoned off from mainstream video exhibitors. In those days many of the mainstream conventioneers would sneak through the hallways to ogle the porn actresses and exhibitionists who annually attended and manned the booths. The adult gathering eventually got so popular that it spawned its own show, which runs in January each year. The AEE is now the place where distributors of every genre of the adult video industry make their deals, show-case their existing stable of stars, and introduce new starlets. It is a company's major marketing connection with viewers, distributors, and retailers. The AVN Awards are annually held on the Saturday evening before the show's closing day.

As my friend and I enter the AEE showroom, there is a small crowd hovering around a porn celebrity at a front booth. It is none other Ron Jeremy, who has appeared in nearly 2000 hard-core videos and is as recognizable among male porn stars as Marilyn Chambers is among females. With 225 pounds spread generously over his five-foot-six inch frame, and as the joke goes, "more chins than a Chinese phone book," Jeremy hardly looks like the prototypical stud who would be in de-mand for x-rated work. He even admits, "I look more like your pizza delivery boy." But there's one part of his body that does fit the bill. His penis is long enough, and his belly at one time was flat enough, that he could actually fellate himself. He per-formed the feat in one of his early movies in the mid 1980s, and actor/comic Eddie Murphy was so impressed by the stunt that he included it in a concert routine that I attended at the Las Vegas Hilton.

> *"If I could suck my own dick, would I?" (long pause) "Damn right!"*
>
> —EDDIE MURPHY

Murphy posed the question, "If I could suck my own dick, would I?" (*long pause*) "Damn right!"

And the audience howled.

Jeremy's acting ability was so far superior to the average male porn star — who couldn't earn a walk-on role in civic theater — that, aug-mented by his generous endowment and his ability to perform on cue, it earned him an inordinate amount of work in the days when story lines and plots were more common in adult feature films.

As we start to visit, he seems almost apologetic, in the presence of my actor friend, that he's never been able to find the mainstream work he dreamed of as a boy. He tells me that he has his Screen Actors Guild card and that he's had parts in five films from the noted late director John Frankenheimer. In each, the credits list his real name, Ron Hyatt. I learn later that he actually flew to France to appear in the Robert DeNiro action thriller *Ronin*, but when his scene was previewed back in the states, several people in the audience recognized him from his sex films and started laughing, so Frankenheimer had to cut the scene.

> "I guess once you start groaning on camera in a sex film, your credibility is shot."
>
> –RON JEREMY

"To be given the old heave-ho just for being recognized is pretty depressing," he told an interviewer. "I guess once you start groaning on camera in a sex film, your credibility is shot."

When Ron questions me about my background and I tell him I have a masters degree in English, he says he has a masters also, in education, and that like me he used to be a teacher. Through later research I find he's telling the truth. I also learn that his mother was a cryptographer during World War II and his father, who is now retired, is a respected physicist.

Ashlyn Gere, my former student turned porn star, had told me in an earlier interview that she could go out in public generally unrecognized, but that once when she was walking through a hotel lobby with Ron Jeremy, various fans shouted out his name from all around them and one group of young men did the *Wayne's World* bow, bending forward and chanting "We're not worthy! We're not worthy!" Though Jeremy didn't achieve the acting career he dreamed of, he did attain cult celebrity status, albeit for an industry that middle America likes to pretend doesn't exist — at least until they get home to their VCRs or cable channels.

Ron can be seen regularly these days on cable, seated at a desk in a talk show infomercial, promoting a penile enhancement product. No doubt he's strategizing how he can become the David Letterman of the x-rated world.

I notice other male porn actors roaming the aisles of the convention, and although their faces and naked bodies appear on posters adorning many booths, and their sweaty bodies and rippling muscles can be viewed on television monitors throughout the room, they appear to be unappreciated by the crowd. Perhaps there is a segment of the gay population that appreciates the looks and sexual capabilities of the male adult actors, but it's clear that in the world of adult video the big bucks and celebrity status is reserved for females only.

The only true male superstar in the adult film genre died of AIDS at age 43 in 1988. John Holmes is said to have had sex with over 10,000 women, and according to a website chronicling his accomplishments, he made 2,274 pornographic films, or about one every three days for 20 years. It's no wonder that the 1981 documentary about his life was titled *Exhausted.*

Holmes, *aka* Johnny Wadd, was as famous for the length of his manhood, 13 inches, as for his durability. His acting ability was nil. Whenever the camera would pull back to show his face during a sex act he would grimace like a man with an abscessed tooth. But the mere fact of his size and endurance has made him a legend, and

Hollywood has not forgotten him. When he died his obituary appeared in the *New York Times*. He is the only male porn star ever to earn that distinction, and his story provided the central plot points for the critically acclaimed *Boogie Nights*, which portrayed the adult-film world to a mainstream audience.

Hollywood last year released a feature film about Holmes, called *Wonderland*, which starred Val Kilmer, that addressed Holmes' role in the 1981 Wonderland Murders, a drug-related massacre in which four people were murdered at the home of reputed cocaine trafficker Eddie Nash. In June 1982 Holmes was acquitted of involvement, although police said his bloody handprint was lifted from a bed where one corpse was found. And after his death, Holmes' widow Sharon told the *L.A.Times* that her husband had admitted to her he helped set up the crime and witnessed the killings. He said he was splattered with blood as he watched three people (whom he did not name) beat five people, killing two men and two women.

While there were other early male porn stars like Richard Pacheco and John Leslie who did possess a measure of acting ability, it remains clear that the only essential requirements for a stud in the adult film business are size, stamina, and the ability to ejaculate on time, and under budget.

As Ron Jeremy is drawn away by autograph seekers and shutterbugs, my friend and I move to another booth where veteran porn star Nina Hartley is signing autographs and posing for some fan photos. She's wearing fishnet stockings and little else from the waist down and each time the fan is about to take a photograph she turns 45 degrees so her rear end faces the camera. She has several times been voted the honor by her peers of having "the best butt in the business," and the savvy performer understands the exact pose her fans want to show their friends back home.

I introduce myself and thank her for an earlier phone interview she gave me about Ashlyn Gere. Nina is a pleasant woman, clearly in the twilight of her career, but she has made a good living for 20 years by aggressively marketing herself and selling her knowledge of sexuality through instructional videotapes and paraphernalia. Hartley is a registered nurse by education, and when she talks about sex she does so with a nurse's awareness of the body and its needs and desires. She previously lived for years with a man and woman whom she referred to as "my husband and wife." In recent years she says she has settled down with a good man. "This is a better situation for me," she says. "I'm very happy now."

> *"I just knew I wanted to spend my time in rooms full of naked people," she says. "And if I could make a living at it, that would be very cool."*
>
> –NINA HARTLEY

When I ask her how her parents have dealt with her career, she tells me that both her mother and father are Buddhist priests.

"They were ordained in 1977 and live in the San Francisco area," she says. "They have never, nor will they ever approve of my life choices, but they have come to a form of acceptance."

Throughout her career, Nina has been an intelligent and plain-spoken advocate of her open sexuality, and is frequently asked to appear on talk shows or at university forums about her career. Next to Marilyn Chambers, Hartley probably has the longest running performing career of any adult film actress.

"I've stayed because this business sustains me," she says. "It is a discipline for me and a path to self-knowledge and spiritual understanding. I'm a bisexual exhibitionist who likes to have sex with a variety of people in front of others and not get arrested. So the adult film world was the only place for me to go to live out those fantasies."

Hartley says the first time she watched an adult film, she knew in her heart that this was the business for her. "I just knew I wanted to spend my time in rooms full of naked people," she says. "And if I could make a living at it, that would be very cool."

Nina was arrested in Las Vegas in 1994 for performing a live-sex show in front of a paid audience. The charges were bargained down to a misdemeanor a year later, and Hartley dismisses the incident as "strictly a political move. It was part of one of those clean-up-Las-Vegas moves that occur every few years," she says. "But who are they kidding? This city was built on sex. Just look around."

In a later interview, Clark County Sheriff Bill Young remembers the episode this way: "Some guy erected a tent in a parking lot near Industrial Road the week that the adult convention was in town. And he got all these porno stars like Nina and Christi Canyon and some others to do a show on stage. They had no business license, they were serving booze, and they had a fifty-dollar cover charge to get in. Hundreds of men showed up, but unfortunately for the promoter a bunch of us were vice cops."

Young says the evening started off innocently enough, "but it got to where guys were going up onstage and porn stars were blowing them . . . all sorts of sex acts. It was a good bust. I remember it made the national news."

Chapter 1

Hartley tells me that very few young adult film actresses can stay in the business for long. "Nobody comes into this thinking they can make a career of it," she says. "But I've found that it's the place where I find my greatest personal satisfaction. Too many girls come into this business for reasons of self-abuse, and they find that the profession can foster those feelings of inadequacy. But they don't stay long. Too many suffer from self-esteem issues or jealous boyfriend issues.

"In my case sex always made me feel good about myself rather than not good about myself. It's all about consent, consent, consent. I knew I loved sex but I didn't want to pick up guys because that's too dangerous, and I didn't want to get hurt. I'm a feminist, a self-aware person first and foremost, and a nurse. When people are sick they need a nurse's care. We need to have people in our culture who are not afraid of sex anymore, who have made their peace with it, who have an understanding of it and can share their knowledge of it. And I enjoy doing that."

> *"The difference between us and Hollywood is money and ego."*
>
> –JANE HAMILTON

Hartley says that the biggest change she has seen in her industry in the last 10 years is the emergence of women as a consumer class purchasing or renting adult films and pornography, separate from their boyfriends. "Women today will decide who they like on their own. They'll like a certain director or actor or actress. They no longer just cop out and say, 'Bring home whatever you like, Honey.'"

It occurs to me as we end our visit that Nina Hartley has given as much to the adult film business as she has received, and that she is as close to being a natural for the industry as anyone I've met.

In another booth close by, I bump into Jane Hamilton, a well-liked and highly regarded executive at VCA, one of the larger adult companies. I introduce myself and remind her that she had done a long phone interview with me about Ashlyn Gere a few months before. Jane is pretty, extremely friendly, and one of the most knowledgeable and admired people in the porn business, having started in the late 1970s as a headlining performer called Veronica Hart. After a brief hiatus from the business, during which time she got married and had two sons, she turned to the production side, and now specializes in making adult films for couples and women. Hamilton, like Gere, is a graduate of the UNLV theater arts department, who has on occasion returned to the Black Box Theatre on campus to appear in university plays. While a student, she had performed in plays by Pinter and Lorca; her professors generally considered her the best actress in the school. In May 2001 Hamilton was profiled in the *New York Times Magazine* by columnist Frank Rich. She told Rich in an interview: "The difference between us and Hollywood is money and ego. We deal with thousands of dollars, not millions. In mainstream films, people are more cutthroat and pumped up about themselves. We're just like regular people — it has to do with exposing yourself. If you show something this intimate, there isn't a lot you can hide behind. You're a little more down to earth."

Jane, now 48, plays the name game with me after I mention several people that we know in common. She then explains to me how she got into the adult business. "I graduated from UNLV in 1975 at age 19, with a degree in theater arts," she says, "and I knew I wanted to be in the entertainment business. I was a very highly sexed girl. I tried the music business for a while, had a few extra parts in mainstream films like *Going in Style*, with George Burns and Art Carney, but then discovered through some responses to my modeling resume that I could be a lead in adult movies and have great sex along with it. It wasn't a tough call for me at all."

As I'm visiting with Jane, she is approached by a tall, extremely slender person wearing a Little Bo Peep costume, complete with powder-blue fringed miniskirt, white hose, high heels, and a walking cane. A closer look reveals that it is a man, or at least was. After a brief visit, he moves on. Jane notices the surprised look on my face. "She's a tranny," she says. "Nice person." As my eyes follow Bo Peep, Jane can't resist a tease. "Nice legs, huh?"

When I get home that night, I discover in my bag of handouts the most recent issue of *Adult Video News*, with a cover story titled "Directors Roundtable." In it are featured the proponents of what the magazine calls New School Porn, videos that feature rough material, like bathroom antics and men clearly dominating women. It's generally meaner, nastier viewing fare than more conventional porn and has little or no plot. Jane Hamilton doesn't like this new material one bit. She feels it's demeaning to women and lowers the bar considerably for the entire adult industry. At one point in the dialogue she says to a gathering of New School directors, "…I want to make stuff that puts out good messages. Even when the chick wants it big and bad and hard, and she wants to be taken by a bunch of guys, it's very clear in my movies that it's *her* wish. I'm not sending out the message to a bunch of guys that it's okay to go out and abuse chicks. And I think that's really dangerous shit to put out there."

Hamilton's view matches mine to the tee, and I think UNLV should be proud to have her as an alumna, even if they're not about to put her face on the cover of their recruiting pamphlets.

As my friend and I move through the aisles another recognizable face approaches. I am introduced to Ivan Nagy, a well-dressed and distinguished looking man in his 60s, sort of a Robin Leach look-alike. His 15 minutes of fame occurred when Heidi Fleiss was busted as the Beverly Hills Madam in the mid 90s. Ivan was Heidi's boyfriend through the period of time when she was booking pricey young call girls for Hollywood's rich and famous. A documentary about Fleiss called *Heidi Fleiss: Hollywood Madam*, produced by a British film company in 1996, features their stormy romantic relationship and how they turned on each other as law enforcement officials ratcheted up the heat. Nagy tells us that was a rough period of time for him, as he was implicated in a pandering role. But he tells us things are great now, and that he is back producing films. His resume lists about a dozen credits producing horror films and low-budget independent features. With him is an attractive woman in her 40s, who appears to be his girlfriend.

We move along to other booths, and I am introduced to Steve Lane, who with his wife, adult actress Serenity, owns a company called Las Vegas Novelties. Their business is selling sex toys and marital aids from a factory in Las Vegas and over the Internet. Steve tells me that business is good, and that he has a great group of product endorsers. In addition to his wife he has Christi Lake (who endorses a vibrator called The Decathalete, which has 10 speeds and is "guaranteed to please"), and Jacklyn Lick, a perky brunette from Portland, Oregon, who enthusiastically offers me a free sample of The Pulsator, her wireless cock ring, which, when placed over the penis, vibrates like crazy.

Chapter 1

"Try it," she says, with a big grin.

"I'm afraid it might short out my pacemaker," I say.

"Ah, you're blushing," she says. "That's cute."

Jacklyn has made over 250 films, mostly in the bondage and light bondage category. "I was really into bondage before I got into films," she says. "I really enjoy it and there's a big audience for it."

In an interview posted on her website, Jacklyn explains that her first inkling that bondage could be enjoyable occurred when she was just 12 years old. "I remember sitting in a car, and the seatbelt was on me sort of tightly," she says. "We were driving down the road, and I placed my hands underneath the seatbelt and thought about struggling to get out. I remember my mom looking over and asking 'What in the heck are you doing?'"

Later on, as a young adult, she says, she liked the feeling of being tied in ropes because "It made me completely ready to please my partner. I think part of it is the excitement of what they are going to do next. Where is he going to touch me? How is he going to touch me? I love that."

> "Ms. Lick is a great employee, very reliable and enthusiastic."
>
> —STEVE LANE

Steve Lane tells me that Ms. Lick is "a great employee, very reliable and enthusiastic and she really believes in the products she endorses." Some of the others are are "Jacklyn's Whack Attack," which is a spanking paddle; a strap-on dildo, which she says "works really great," and a set of holiday greeting cards posing with his majesty Ron Jeremy.

Jacklyn has been to Australia twice in the last four months for Las Vegas Novelties, and on a recent business trip to Estonia, a small country between Russia and Latvia, she went into a novelty store and found several of the products she endorses. "Our toys are all over the world," she says. "We have a great company, and it's growing like crazy."

Between making bondage films, which she has cranked out at a pace of about three per month over the last seven years, Jacklyn is going to college, pursuing a double major in psychology and human health. She makes dozens of appearances on the road as a feature dancer, she studies herbology and makes a lot of her own household products that are toxin-free, and she is a spokesmodel for PETA, the animal protection group. She's also been a vegetarian since she was 13.

"She won't eat meat but she loves to beat meat," my friend says. I tell him his joke is so bad that I'm going to include it in the book and tell everybody who groans in response the name of the person who told it.

"Go ahead," he says. "I'll deny that I even know you."

There are two gay porn booths at the Adult Entertainment Expo, but on the day of our visit, which is the opening day of the show, neither is doing much business. My feeling is that an industry this permissive has an innate desire to serve all tastes and preferences, but that while lesbianism is encouraged and is a staple in adult films, male homosexuality is a persuasion totally unto itself. You never see male sexual activity even as an incidental activity in a "regular" adult video. Christi Lake explains that while the gay industry generates big money, this convention doesn't draw many gays.

"Part of it is that they have their own conventions," she says. "There's even a Gay *Adult Video News* awards show at a different time of year." Christi says that the adult industry does more than tolerate the gay crowd. "I think we accept them totally," she says. "They represent a large part of expressing sexuality."

There is also a booth featuring Big Girls, those with breast measurements of 48 inches and beyond, and cup sizes that go into the later letters of the alphabet. A segment of the fan base is totally devoted to these plus-size stars, and when the two models staffing the booth are asked to pose, they unhesitatingly unleash mammoth breasts from their tank tops and give ear-to-ear grins. One of the girls winces as she struggles to reinsert her breasts under her shirt. It looks very painful.

The biggest autograph line by far is for Jenna Jameson. It's two wide and about 60 people deep at 3 in the afternoon. There's no question that Jenna is the biggest star in this booming industry. She has been featured in mainstream movies like Howard Stern's *Private Parts*; has hosted the popular cable series "Wild on....." that examines racy events around the world; has posed for acclaimed photographers like Annie Leibowitz, David LaChapelle, and Timothy Greenfield-Sanders; and was the recent subject of a two-hour documentary on the E! Channel. In that documentary, we learned that Jenna was going to be married the following month and wanted to start a family, but would continue to pour her energy into her lucrative website, Club Jenna.

We also learned that Jenna Jameson got her start in the adult world by dancing nude in Las Vegas clubs when she was just 17 years old, while she was still attending Bonanza High School here. It appears that Jenna has come full circle back home, and her appearance at the adult video convention and later at the Porn Oscars is but one more reminder that when it comes to adult entertainment and what some like to call "acceptable sin," all roads do indeed lead through Las Vegas.

B-Student in an X-Rated World

"Take even the low-end $10 billion estimate, and pornography is a bigger business than professional football, basketball and baseball put together. People pay more money for pornography in America in a year than they do on movie tickets, more than they do on all the performing arts combined."

— FRANK RICH, NEW YORK TIMES MAGAZINE, MARCH 22, 2002

It was 1980, the first day of the fall semester in English 101 at UNLV. Thirty 18- and 19-year-olds sat stone-faced. My basic composition class, required of all college freshmen, was as popular as a visit to an oral surgeon. I would be assigning a short in-class essay to get a feel for the talent, or lack thereof, that I would be molding over the next four months. The writing exercise was also my way of discouraging plagiarism: if several weeks later a student turned in a homework assignment that read like an Anna Quindlen thought piece, I could refer back to the sample essay and explain that as great a teacher as I was, I was incapable of bringing any student that far, that fast.

As I was writing my name on the blackboard and informing the students that, because I was just a few years older than they, it was permissible to address me by my first name, I heard the click, click, click of pointed heels on the tile floor. I paused and turned to see who was making the late entrance. It was a dazzling young woman with short brown hair. She gave me a sheepish smile and shrugged her shoulders. "Sorry" she said, "I couldn't find the room."

> ## Thirty 18- and 19-year-olds sat stone-faced.

She coyly slid into a front-seat desk. She was wearing hermetically-sealed jeans and a gold waist-chain. In the interest of maintaining teacher-student decorum, I did my best to act unimpressed. My eighteen-year-old male students weren't as restrained. One of them actually whistled, which drew some giggles.

Hers was the first essay I read when I returned to my office after class. The topic was "My Dream Career." She wrote about wanting to become an actress, and how one day she would make her mark in Hollywood.

Chapter 2

There's no denying she became a film star. But with a slight twist.

To her thousands of fans who faithfully rent or buy her movies or subscribe to her website or pay a cover charge to see her dance, and to the members of her genre who have elected her to their Hall of Fame, Ashlyn Gere is a major star. But she rarely gets stopped in shopping malls for an autograph, and even those who do recognize her are probably reluctant to admit it. That's because she's a legend in an industry that has never been able to elevate itself much beyond a whisper and a giggle.

My former UNLV student, you see, is a porn star.

How she came to be one of the most popular actresses ever to have wild sex on camera, and how for over a decade she has sustained a career in an industry that chews up and spits out most young women in a year or two, interested me both personally and professionally. Despite the fact that she was irresistibly cute and demurely sexy as a student at UNLV, and popular enough to be a four-year cheerleader for the Runnin' Rebel teams of the Jerry Tarkanian glory years, I never would have guessed that of the hundreds of students I taught in my five years in front of a classroom *she* would be the one to pursue porno as a career. She was just too bubbly and innocent. After one semester she gave me a coffee mug with the name "Brillo" inscribed on it, a clear reference to my being a white man with a bad Afro. I kidded her that it was too late for apple-polishing, that the final grades had been turned in. She said, "Oh, whatever grade I get is fine. I just wanted you to know that I enjoyed the class."

I could maybe have seen her becoming a marketing rep for a large company, or even a television anchorwoman. But an acrobatic and totally uninhibited sex goddess? Never.

"Ashlyn was the most conservative one among us," says Chris Richards, a Las Vegas children's dance troop leader and one of her closest friends from their UNLV cheerleading days. [Gere will allow use of her stage name only, although her friends always use her real name in talking about her.] "She was always shy around guys, even though they were always crazy about her. And she certainly wasn't promiscuous. She had one boyfriend at a time. I remember once we were at a party and this guy she really liked was there. I urged her to go over and talk with him, but she wouldn't do it. Fear of rejection, I guess."

> ## "Obviously, they don't use body doubles in those films."
>
> — HEIDI

Another friend and fellow Rebel cheerleader, Heidi Hopper, who today owns a local dance studio, says, "She had done some small parts in low-budget, thriller-type movies, and I knew how badly she wanted to be an actress and how hard she'd trained for it. But when I heard she was making adult films, I didn't believe it. I thought she must have used a body double. That shows how naïve I was.

"Obviously," Heidi says with a big laugh, "they don't use body doubles in those films."

It may come as a surprise that these pom-pom buddies of Ashlyn's, now doting mothers and career women, still remain close to her.

"We talk all the time," Heidi says. "I don't think she's changed much from college. She just has this outrageous job. She even asked me once if I would carry her baby for her as a surrogate mother. I

Chapter 2

think she would have made a great mom. She's very maternal. I do miss spending more time with her because she travels a lot and we all tend to hang out with the people we work with. But on special occasions, like birthdays or baby showers, she's always invited. She dresses conservatively and fits right in and everyone likes her."

"But does it cause a stir when she arrives?" we wonder.

"Usually a few of the women know about her career, but most don't," Heidi says.

Those looking for a story about the quintessential Las Vegas girl raised in Sin City who inevitably gives in to the temptations of the flesh may be disappointed. Nor is the story of Ashlyn Gere a morality tale of a pretty girl who took the easy road and lived to regret it.

After 13 years of being a star in a business that's grown so big and profitable that the *New York Times* recently called pornography "no longer a sideshow to mainstream [entertainment], but the new mainstream," Ashlyn offers no apologies.

"You may find my story boring," she says, "because I don't have any horror stories about the adult business. My years in it fulfilled a certain need I had for attention. I love sex, and I learned to enjoy it thoroughly on camera. And I'm going to retire soon from films with absolutely no regrets."

She pauses for a minute, then makes a concession. "I know the majority of girls who appear in these films couldn't say that, but I can."

So how did Ashlyn Gere become . . . well, *Ashlyn Gere?* How did the Las Vegas born-and-raised cutie, girl-next-door cheerleader, good student, the UNLV theater arts and communications graduate, become one of Hollywood's best bad girls?

"I guess you could say I got on the bus, and this is where it took me," she says, sitting cross-legged in a chair in her comfortable Summerlin home. She's wearing jeans and a t-shirt, no makeup, and her dark hair is pulled back. She looks just like the girl in my English class, only 20 years older, but with the same infectious smile, sparkly eyes, and porcelain complexion. Her voice is slightly huskier than I remembered it, due no doubt to the occasional cigarette breaks she takes during our conversation.

Her husband, Layne Parker (his working name), who directs adult films and is totally supportive and proud of her career, is in the other room. I've known him casually for a dozen or so years, and when he passes through he greets me warmly. Layne also went to UNLV, played football there, and worked as a cameraman and news producer for a local television station, which is where we met. A 130-pound Rottweiler, who Ashlyn calls "my baby," never wanders far from her side. I sense that between her husband and her dog, she has all the security she'll ever need.

Ashlyn begins to recount the two decades since she earned grades of "B" in both semesters of my freshman English class. She tells of a quick marriage shortly after college that ended in less than a year, and how she then went to Los Angeles to chase her dream of a film career. For moral and financial support, her mother actually moved with her, and shared an apartment. Ashlyn quickly got her Screen Actors Guild card, but was unable to get a top-flight manager.

She was eventually signed by an agent who specialized in teenage actors. He sent her on dozens of auditions, and with her youthful look she frequently read for teen roles of characters years younger than her actual age.

"I often heard back from casting agents that I read so well for these small parts that they didn't want to cast me opposite the bigger roles because I would make the lead actors look bad," she says. "It was never an outright rejection, but rather these long excuses why I didn't get the part."

About a dozen other graduates of UNLV's theater department went to L.A. at about the same time, looking to break in, and Ashlyn was the only one who even got a job in theater. The others either waited tables or were unemployed.

Her job was dressing actors for small stage plays — and other behind-the-scenes work — and she remembers helping people like Bill Pullman and Phillip Baker Hall. "I watched carefully every night and was trying to improve my craft," she says, "and I took a lot of acting classes, the whole deal. I'd been in several college plays at UNLV, so I was capable."

Eventually, she landed some sizable roles in low-budget horror films, and became something of a scream queen. Her credit list includes titles like *Creepozoids*, *Dream Maniac*, *Evil Laugh*, and *Missing Children*. A video viewer's guide that critiques films of the last 30 years gave *Creepozoids* a "one-turkey" rating and offered this capsule review: "A post-apocalyptic sci-fi horror yarn about military deserters who find an abandoned science lab that has a bloodthirsty monster wandering the halls. A waste of time."

Ashlyn recalls she was paid only fifty dollars a day for these non-union movies. But at least she was on camera delivering lines, and even Jack Nicholson had to make several low-grade biker films before he broke out in *Easy Rider*. But the big break she was hoping for never came, and she grew increasingly disillusioned with casting-couch proposals.

"It angers me that I was never told about the sleazy side of Hollywood," she says, her voice rising. "It seemed I got hit on every time I went for an audition. It makes me mad thinking about it even now."

After three lean years, she moved back to Las Vegas and took a job at a McCarran Airport car rental agency. "I was bored to tears," she says, "but I felt like I'd hit the wall in L.A." She started dating Layne and, like more couples than would care to admit, they watched the occasional adult video together. "I would always dissect the acting," she says. "Obviously, men don't watch sex films for the drama, but I couldn't help thinking that I could take that industry by storm."

> ## "Obviously, men don't watch sex films for the drama . . ."
>
> –Ashlyn Gere

That notion lay dormant until, out of the blue, a *Penthouse* magazine photographer who knew of her film work approached her with an offer at a time when her money and self-esteem were low. Layne thought the *Penthouse* layout was a good idea, and Ashlyn admits she was hungry to be in the limelight again. She posed for the pictures and just three months later, in 1989, the magazine ran an eight-page layout of her and put her on the cover of some of its European editions. The accompanying text told of her acting credits, and even mentioned her cheerleading days at UNLV.

While *Penthouse* shows full-frontal nudity, Ashlyn was not uncomfortable with it. She doesn't deny being an exhibitionist. "As

Chapter 2

a cheerleader, I always loved being in front of a huge crowd," she admits. "That's the thrill of it, having people watch you." Knowing that her parents would hear about the nude pictures, she showed the magazine to them when it first came out.

"I remember my mom saying, 'These are beautiful pictures, honey, but you don't want to do any more of this.'"

Her father, who died two years ago, just smiled. "He was always proud of me," she says, the pain of his loss still evident in her eyes.

Ashlyn earned abut four thousand dollars for the photo shoot, about two months' wages at her day job. Shortly after the magazine came out, a small-time adult-video director invited her to Los Angeles to appear in one of his movies.

"I talked it over for a long time with Layne," she says, "and he was fine with it. But the first time I drove to L.A. to shoot some scenes, I couldn't go through with it. I went to the guy's house and as he talked on the phone, he said, 'Let me show you what I shot yesterday,' and he put in a tape. I broke down in tears and drove home the same day. And that was that. It just freaked me out."

A few months later, back in Las Vegas and increasingly bored with her car rental job, Ashlyn decided to give the adult scene another try. She had heard about Jim South, owner of World Modeling Agency, and how he handled most of the bigger stars in the adult world. He took one look at her and signed her up. Being a *Penthouse* girl gave Ashlyn instant status in his world.

"In any industry, there are different levels," she says. "And there are definitely back alleyways in the adult world, but with Jim South I was at least getting in at the very top."

Ashlyn discovered that women in porn are paid on three levels. An "A" girl has a beautiful face and a great figure and is featured on the box cover of the video that is sold to consumers and rented at video stores. A "B" girl has either a great face or figure, but not both, and is less often featured on a box cover. And a "C" girl is a "filler" actress, usually doing one or two scenes in a movie, often with multiple partners. The pay varies greatly.

As an instant "A" girl, Ashlyn started by making about $750 per scene, and appeared on nearly every box cover. As her following and reputation as one of the industry's hottest stars grew through the 90s, her payment for scenes increased to as much as $10,000 per scene.

> *". . . a top girl will make between $10,000 to $25,000 per movie . . ."*
>
> —Ashlyn Gere

"I don't want to divulge my salary," she says, "but a top girl will make between $10,000 to $25,000 per movie, which might be two scenes and a box cover. And there are a couple girls today, like Jenna Jameson (also raised in Las Vegas), who make far more than that."

The key is to become a hot enough property that having your name on a film guarantees immediate sales. Marilyn Chambers was the first adult star to gain a huge following, and through the '90s, Ashlyn was clearly in the top five. Her films include *Chameleons: Not the Sequel* (considered by some a cult classic), *Put It in Gere*, *Club Sin*, and *Crime and Passion*.

For a professional assessment of her work, I spoke with the man who launched her career in porn. Jim South has for two decades pulled back the curtain to the adult film world for hundreds of pretty young girls. Most don't last long, on average a year or two. Ashlyn, he says, is one of the very few who enter the porn world with eyes wide open.

"Ashlyn Gere is one of the best actresses ever in this industry," South told me. "On sheer acting ability, I would rate her a 10. And she's a very nice lady as well, a total professional, always on time, a class act. She's one of the very few who can handle dialogue and create a believable character, so when an adult film director is shooting a movie that has some real plot, she is on the short list. But of course, she's very hot in the sheets as well. She totally gets into the sex scenes and her audience knows it. Nobody's that good an actress to completely fake it."

Adult film director Jane Hamilton, another porn Hall of Famer who starred in dozens of films under the name Veronica Hart, and who coincidentally is also a graduate of the UNLV Theater Department, also has high praise for Ashlyn.

> *"She totally gets in the sex . . . Nobody's that good an actress to completely fake it."*
>
> –JIM SOUTH

"She's at the top as an adult film actress," Jane says. "Probably in the top 10 or 15 ever. Ashlyn is a real actress as opposed to a girl who just has sex on camera. I think it's because she had her feet on the ground and carefully considered the decision before entering the business."

Hamilton was also considered a legitimate actress in an industry that will readily accept robotic acting and botched lines if the package is desirable. From her UNLV training, Jane knew how to deliver dialogue and how to develop character. She is also a delightful and funny interview. "I must tell you there are people in our industry that, thank God they can get paid for doing it on camera, because they couldn't hold down a job at McDonald's," she says.

I couldn't resist asking Jane about what it means to have two sex film Hall of Famers coming from the same university.

"It's kind of a private joke in Las Vegas that the two most famous graduates of the theater arts school are adult-film stars," she says. "I'm pretty sure they don't use it as a recruiting tool."

Porn veteran Nina Hartley says that Ashlyn has succeeded in the adult business because "She is a gorgeous brunette in a world of all blondes. She's classy looking, with a great body, and knows how to tear it up in bed." Hartley categorizes her as "slightly more sophisticated than the girl next door, but certainly wholesome."

Okay, so my former student has made a great living in a hush-hush business, has managed to sustain a long-term relationship with a husband who is totally accepting and supportive of her career choices, and is seemingly at peace with her life. I still can't help wondering what it takes to perform the most intimate of acts in a room full of strangers, and for all the world to see? I mean, what is the thought process that allows someone to do this?

"Answering all these questions is as hard as your English class," Ashlyn says. She rocks back and forth in her chair, quietly formulating her answer.

"Look, I do think there's a wonderful place in many couples' lives, or an individual's life, for adult movies. Whether that's keeping wackos off the street or adding spice to the bedroom or helping couples with sexual ideas to keep their marriage fresh, there are positive reasons for sex films to exist.

"But I got involved because after being frustrated in the mainstream acting business and having a job I hated; the way I looked at it was that having an adult script in my hand was better than having no script at all. Certainly, if I could change everything and have three of Demi Moore's roles, I'd do it in a minute. Because that was my goal when I first went to L.A. But that was not available to me, so I took the opportunities that came my way and I have no regrets. Some of these girls do it strictly for the money; others think it would be a lark to make a movie, and others just love sex. None of them last very long. Then there are a few like me who want a little fame and think they'd be good at it, and who treat it like a professional business and turn it into a good career."

Although she doesn't cut quite to the heart of my question, I let it be. Because, despite the fact that both of us have moved on to different careers and different challenges, she is still a girl who once learned a thing or two from me in a classroom, and that teacher-student distance remains. I'm sure if you asked her, she'd say it's much easier to have sex on film with a total stranger and a dozen crew members watching than to answer probing questions from a man who used to be her English instructor. (In fact, she initially declined my requests for an interview.)

> *"Whether that's keeping wackos off the street or adding spice to the bedroom . . . there are positive reasons for sex films to exist."*
>
> –Ashlyn Gere

Ironically, it is through her sex stardom that Ashlyn finally did get a break in legitimate films. Among her legion of mostly closeted fans was Glenn Morgan, producer of the *X-Files*, who hired her for a small part in the James Wong film, *The One*, starring Jet Li. And last year she won a much larger part that required a month of shooting in Canada for a sequel to the film *Willard*, about a boy and his rat. She holds her own in that one with R. Lee Ermey (*Full Metal Jacket*), Crispin Glover (*Back to the Future, Charlie's Angels*), and Laura Herring (*Mulholland Drive*). In neither film was she asked to remove her clothes.

"Can you imagine," she says, "that after being naked in over 100 movies, I got some legitimate acting parts and they never once asked me to get naked? In one respect, it's very flattering, but in another way, I'm almost insulted."

Chapter 2

A World Away From Minnesota

"…When she was good,
She was very, very good,
But when she was bad she was horrid."

— HENRY WADSWORTH LONGFELOW

In the late 1980s a young woman named Christi was employed at a large hearing aid factory in Minnesota. Her job was pouring acrylic liquid to form molds for earpieces. It was the same material that is used to make acrylic fingernails, only more durable. The fumes from the liquid smelled horrible, and Christi had a growing and uneasy feeling that constant exposure to the toxic materials was detrimental to her health, but she was making $11 an hour and had been promoted past most of the men in her department because of her speed and efficiency. In her eight years on the job at Qualitone, she had the lowest return rate on custom-fit earpieces, and her bosses appreciated her reliability.

"I didn't hate the job at all; in fact I kind of liked it," Christi says. "And eleven bucks an hour back then was pretty good for a woman in a factory job, so I hung in there. It was the type of place where people worked their entire careers. I figured I'd be there for at least 20 years, so I could qualify for the retirement plan, cash in on the good ol' 401K and all that."

Christi recounts her work history as she sips coffee on the patio of a restaurant in Henderson. She is wearing a Minnesota Twins warm-up jacket and baseball cap and not a hint of makeup. "But then in a short period of time three people in the plant were diagnosed with cancer," she says, "and one of them, who was a good friend of mine, died. I expressed my concerns about the health standards, and the plant management said that OSHA had said everything was fine and aboveboard, but I didn't believe it. I started looking for a way to get out of that life."

Christi had been living on her own since she graduated from high school. Her parents had tired of the long cold winters in Minnesota and had moved to a warmer valley climate in Utah, where her father had family members. Christi elected to stay in the Land of the Lakes (eventually taking the trademark of her home state for her stage name), and she enjoyed her independence. She had a steady boyfriend and, with her decent paying job, could come and go as she pleased. Although she describes herself as a tomboy growing up, and still dresses the part today, she had no inhibitions about sex.

Christi's mother had given her the birds-and-bees talk at age nine when she had her first period, and she was sexually active as a teenager. Her mother once caught her with condoms and a spermicidal in her roller-skating case, and rather than chastise her she made certain Christi was well versed. "She didn't want me to submit to urban legends like 'the Coca-Cola douche' to prevent conception," she says. "My parents knew they couldn't prevent me from having sex, but they could protect me from an unwanted pregnancy. They took a practical approach to it."

Even before Christi left the hearing-aid factory, she had made a few extra dollars competing in amateur topless dancing contests. With her long shapely legs and outgoing personality, she found a confidence onstage that belied an innate shyness. She even invited several of the men who worked at the factory to come down and cheer for her in her first competition, at the Solid Gold Gentlemen's Club in Minneapolis.

> *"I think seven of them came down and yelled like crazy for me. I finished second and won a hundred dollars.*
>
> —Christi Lake

"I think seven of them came down and yelled like crazy for me. I finished second and won a hundred dollars. And then a few months after that the plant manager called me in and told me he didn't think it was a good idea that I enter these contests because what if I turned around one day and accused one of the men of sexual harassment. He said that would put the company in an awkward position. So I said, 'No problem, I've got a perfect solution. I quit.' And I did."

About this time, in early 1993, Christi's boyfriend took some nude photos of her and submitted them to Gallery men's magazine, in a "Girl Next Door" photo feature. The magazine ran one of the photos and paid her a token fee of $50. That was the symbolic moment of her turning professional.

Christi says that she and her boyfriend from the very beginning had a non-traditional relationship, viewing sex as an enjoyable pastime that didn't have to be exclusive. They had sex with multiple partners and had even participated in a few swinging parties, where mate-swapping was the name of the game.

Later that year, they attended a Lifestyles convention in Las Vegas at the Tropicana Hotel. These gatherings are prime recruiting venues for nude-model photographers and filmmakers, who are always on the hunt for what one of them calls "sweet young things." Christi fit the bill perfectly. She and her girlfriend Sheena, who was also a neophyte in the adult world, were asked to do a 20-minute test photo shoot in a hotel room for a still photographer. The session lasted six hours, and the following day the two were invited by a video company, Arrow Productions, to engage in a nude tennis match. It was billed as Amateurs vs. the Pros. Christi and Sheena took on big-name porn stars Danielle and Nina Hartley in a doubles match. (Not surprisingly, there was no shortage of volunteers to be line judges and ball boys.) After the convention Christi and Sheena flew to New York for a full-fledged magazine shoot.

"The curiosity factor captured my imagination," she says. "It was never about the money, it was never about becoming famous or anything like that. I just found it fun, adventurous, and flattering. I mean I'm not a knockout or some glamour girl. I was the neighborhood babysitter and errand runner. I've always gone around in sweatshirts and jeans, and I never wear makeup unless I'm working. But I was a very sexual person always, and I was bisexual, too, so I was almost irresistibly drawn to a world that put a lot of attention on that."

The pictures she posed for in New York appeared a few months later in two fetish publications, one called Shave and another called Leg Action. While those magazines are not exactly in the category of Reader's Digest or TV Guide when it comes to popular appeal, an entire class of magazines exists for those with very specific, unusual appetites. Whether it's "mature" women in the 50-plus age bracket, obese women, outrageously stacked women, flat women, women who wear stiletto heels and crack whips, gay men with an abundance of body piercings, transsexuals — known in the trade as trannies — or women like Christi with long legs who shave all their pubic hair, there's a segment of the population interested in seeing it.

> *"The curiosity factor captured my imagination,"*
>
> –CHRISTI LAKE

Arrow Productions, the Las Vegas-based production company that had arranged her photo shoots, liked her so much they invited her to the Adult Consumer Electronics Show in 1995 and asked her to sign autographs in their booth. The Arrow people discovered that in addition to being a hot babe on camera, Christi genuinely liked people and was a glib conversationalist. She didn't possess even a hint of the hardness that is often found in young women willing to make the daring leap into the adult film world.

"Appearing at that convention was really cool and fascinating and made me feel good," she says. "And the man I was dating at the time, whose professional name is John Yuma, was also very encouraging and supportive and he was getting a kick out of it as well. He was starting to get into the business from the production side, and we were exploring our sexuality in all kinds of ways. It was at that first convention that people kept handing me cards and wanting me to start shooting videos. The two biggest agents, Jim South and a man who goes by the name Reb, both said that when I was ready I should come out to Los Angeles and they would put me to work."

> ## "It turned out I did over 75 movies that first year."
>
> –Christi Lake

Christi and John talked it over and they thought that as a new girl she could maybe get work in about nine or 10 movies that first year, and then see how it went.

She watched a lot of adult films, and took notes on the actors and actresses she thought were attractive and would be fun to work with.

"It turned out I did over 75 movies that first year," she says. "The business really takes off for new girls, and it's such a whirlwind that you have to have your head on straight to handle it all. That's why so many girls burn out quickly. They get a ton of work the first year because everyone wants to shoot the fresh new face and the hot new body, but unless a girl is in it for the right reasons, and quickly grasps the business side of the adult industry, she'll be gone very quickly."

In the beginning, Christi would usually be required for just one sex scene, with very little dialogue. She says that when a girl is breaking into the business, adult film directors and producers are mainly looking to see if she has any anxiety about it, or whether her nervousness shows on camera. The best performances come from girls who quickly learn where the camera is at all times, yet act totally uninhibited, as though the camera were catching them in totally unguarded wild sex. It's a tricky balance.

"Because my boyfriend and I had had sex with several people in the room as swingers, shooting a video didn't seem that unusual to me," she says. "And because I loved having sex, there wasn't much acting involved. It was all great fun for me. But I quickly grasped the reality of it, that this was all being done for viewing purposes, for men to masturbate and couples to watch and get excited, and that it was both pleasurable and educational at the same time.

"When you're having sex with a guy and are totally into it and the director yells cut and needs to reset the lights or change the film, it can be difficult. The torture of making films is the hot lights and the awkward positions and having an impatient director insist on making you stop a scene when you're really excited. There were times that I would ignore the 'Cut' direction and just keep going. And some directors really didn't like that because they wanted to move right along, chop, chop."

Christi says that the stop-and-start activity in sex scenes is much tougher for the men than the women. "Well, there's the obvious, that the man has to keep a hard-on," she says. "They can't fake being turned on, while we can." And she explains that it's not always comfortable for a heterosexual man to have another guy with a camera crawling between his legs and aiming up at him.

"If a guy is homophobic, he won't last very long because that's just part of the deal," she says.

She adds that situations come up during a DP that are uncomfortable, as well.

"Excuse my ignorance," I say, "but what is a DP?"

"A double penetration," she replies. "One guy on the bottom, the woman on top of him, and a second guy entering her from the rear. When one guy's unit hits the other guy's sometimes they'll get all freaky about it and the girl is lying there in the middle, going 'Would you guys just quit fighting and get on with it, because I'm sitting here getting sore!' That sort of stuff does happen from time to time."

"Doesn't that hurt?" I inquire.

"Yes," she says. "I have relatively small openings, so I'm not beside myself with joy when a guy hung like Secretariat shows up on the set."

> *"I never had one orgasm making a hearing aid," she says.*
> —CHRISTI LAKE

She recalls producing and acting in a scene down in Florida with a man she'd never met, but who was rumored to be especially well endowed. "You know how guys brag," she says, "and I thought Yeah, yeah, we'll see. And then he dropped his shorts and he was huge! I had to call in my friend Chloe to do the scene. The guy was just way too big for me. I like medium- to small-sized men because I can go much longer and it's more fun."

Christi was paid only $300 per scene initially, but she was more than satisfied with the money. It was still a far better wage than the eleven dollars she was making in the hearing-aid factory. "And I never had one orgasm making a hearing aid," she says.

She would learn in time that adult films were a multi-billion dollar industry, and that adult rentals in hotel rooms and sales/rentals from video stores far exceeded profits from mainstream Hollywood features, but she says the money had next to nothing to do with her decision to become a porn star.

"It's really all about the sex for most of us," she says. "That and all the attention, everyone telling you how hot you are. Oh, you can make a nice living out of it, and girls who are considering it as a profession will usually ask me about the money that can be made, but that's not the reason they get into it, either. If a girl's sole motivation for getting into it is to earn a quick buck she'll be out of the business very quickly."

Christi's first significant adult feature was called Fashion Plate and was produced by Vivid Videos and directed by a woman named Toni English. "I was a last minute fill-in for someone who didn't show up," she says, "and they were looking for someone who was a character actor. My scene was with an actor named Drew Drake, and he was exciting to be with, and with all of the energy and adrenalin that was going through my body I could have gone on for hours. I thought it was all very cool."

So did her boyfriend. "John's company started doing well right away," she says, "and it did not require him to be there every day, so he would sometimes come to the set and encourage me and help me. It was a turn-on for him because then we would go home and discuss it and go at it and all that good stuff, which was cool. My doing these films was definitely an enhancement to our sex life."

Our conversation is interrupted by her cell phone, and a reminder from her current long-time boyfriend, who also happens to be named John, that she needs to stop at the store and bring home coffee and butter. "Don't let me forget that," she says. "I'm so forgetful these days." She then holds her hand over the receiver and whispers to me, "I've always dated guys with boring first names. Either John or Bob or Bill. Don't ask me why."

After less than two years of making videos, Christi decided she wanted to try the production end of the business. She and John Yuma produced *Directors' Wet Dreams* and a movie now called *Hollywood Hookers*. It was originally called Southern Comfort, but the alcohol company of the same name sued her for copyright infringement.

"We hired the talent, hired the directors, paid for the script, the whole deal," she says. "The first four movies we made cost around $25,000 each."

While the movies didn't make money in the beginning, profit was generated when Christi sold the rights to the adult giant VCA. She used part of that money to buy her house in Henderson.

About two years into the adult film business, Christi was still doing dance engagements, and she was sent a ticket to fly to Las Vegas to perform at Little Darlings. She took the opportunity to take a stopover flight to Utah to visit her parents. It had bothered her since she entered the business that she hadn't been totally forthcoming with them, so she made the bold decision to tell them exactly what she was doing with her life. Although they knew that she had an open relationship with her boyfriend, and that she had been nude dancing for some time, she was apprehensive about how they would take the news that she was doing sex films.

"I took them to dinner and we had a couple cocktails, and I made sure we opened a bottle of wine when we got back to the house," she says. "I told them that there was something they needed to know and that I couldn't keep it from them any longer. They got very quiet.

"I said, 'I'm doing adult movies.'

"Neither said anything for a while and I said, 'Please someone say something,' and finally my dad said 'I'm not surprised.'

"I started breathing again, and then I said, 'Wait a minute….why are you not surprised?'

"And he said, 'Well, you always were an exhibitionist.'

"And I said, 'I was not. I was a tomboy.'

"My mother's reaction was, 'I was afraid you were going to say you were gay and I was not going to get any grandchildren.'

"I said, 'Well, actually I'm bisexual, Mom, but the grandchildren will have to wait a while because I don't have children in my plans yet.'

"She didn't grasp the bisexual part," Christi says. "It went right over her head. She just heard what she wanted to hear, and that was that grandchildren weren't out of the question. That was all she cared about.

"All along I expected them to say something like, 'You poor child. We're going to take you away from all this.' But part of their understanding was that they had watched adult films together when they were younger. … And I recall my dad saying, 'How could we condemn you for being in something we used to watch ourselves?'

"And then we talked about how long I'd been doing the films and whether there were drugs on the set and a lot of questions like that. I told them the whole truth, that I didn't do drugs at all, and that I hardly ever had a drink and that no one had forced me to do anything that I didn't want to do."

Christi's father Gary, when contacted in Utah, says he does remember being shocked at the news, but adds that he's proud of his daughter for her honesty and he fully supports the decisions she's willingly made with her life.

"I'll tell you that this wouldn't have been my first career choice for her as a father," he says. "But my main concern with anything she does is that she is happy and doing it of her own volition."

Gary and his wife have met several of Christi's friends in the adult business and he says it's surprising what a nice group of people they are. "Of course, just like any segment of society, there are a few assholes in there," he says. The group he finds the weirdest are the fans of the sex industry. "The people who attend the conventions just to get a look at the people making the films . . . now there are some real weirdoes in that group," he says.

> "The people who attend the conventions just to get a look at the people making the films...now there are some real weirdos in that group."
>
> —CHRISTI'S FATHER

Gary's approval of Christi was exhibited a few years ago when he went onstage with his daughter at an event called "Night of the Stars" to help her accept an award she won for her advocacy of free speech and the First Amendment. Christi laughs when she recounts how her dad raised his arms above his head in the Rocky Balboa victory pose as they left the stage.

"I'm quite proud of the fact that my daughter stands up for her beliefs," he says. "She's spoken to MENSA [the high IQ group] about her career, and she's also addressed some college classes. I was more than happy to go onstage with her the night she was honored."

Gary's hunch is that his daughter was pushed into the adult business by her first boyfriend (a claim she takes slight issue with, saying she went very willingly), and that he'll be glad when she retires and gets into another line of work.

"My biggest concern has always been the health issue and a fear that she'd contract AIDS," he says. "No matter how safe you are, and I know she plays it as safe as she can in that business, there are no guarantees that she wouldn't contract it."

"I've been condom-mandatory for the last six years," Christi says, when we move into a discussion of AIDS and how prevalent it is in her industry.

I bring to her attention an article in the Los Angeles Times Magazine by P.J. Huffstutter (Sunday, January 12, 2003) entitled "See No Evil," which reports that a disproportionate number of adult video performers have contracted AIDS and other sexually transmitted diseases. Christi says she's aware of the piece, and that fear of contracting AIDS has always been her number one concern as a performer.

"I'm sympathetic to a point," she says, of the performers who are now HIV-positive or have full-blown AIDS. "But life is all about choices. Some of these people come right off the street and make a film without any testing or asking questions of the other performers. The good video companies like Vivid and VCA require that we have a PCR AIDS test within the last 30 days of any performance. [n.b.: The test is officially called an HIV-1 DNA by PCR test. The initials stand for Polymerase Chain Reaction. It is thought to be the best test available because it goes right into the DNA. As of March 14, 2003, adult performers also require testing for chlamydia and gonorrhea.]

Christi recalls once turning down a job that was to pay her $1,500 for a single scene because the actor she was supposed to work with didn't have current test results. "The test he showed me was 45 days old," she says. "And when I said I needed to see a recent one, he said, 'I don't work that much because I'm mostly producing, and besides, we're using condoms.'

"I told the producers that they'd have to find me another male to work with," she says. "They talked it over for a while, and because this guy had a bigger name at the time than I did and he was their bread and butter, instead of getting rid of him they got rid of me. My time was wasted and I didn't get paid a dime. I thought that was irresponsible."

> "You have to be really horny to do this year after year."
>
> –CHRISTI LAKE

Because the adult industry is unregulated, and no one foresees a time in the near future when the "labor" will become unionized with all the expected benefits that would accompany union membership, actors and actresses will shuffle in and out of the porno world grabbing the money and thrills while they can, until the next pretty face and hard body captures a producer's eye. Christi estimates that the average adult film actress lasts about two years or less in the business. "Anyone who's been in over five years is a veteran," she says, "and someone who has been in eight years or longer, as I have, truly understands the business side of things and isn't kidding anyone about their true motivation. You have to be really horny to do this year after year."

Certain performers in the adult industry carve an unforgettable niche among fans of the genre either for some trademark sexual behavior or for a series of movies in which they do something that's never been done before. An actress named Chloe, for instance, has on-camera orgasms that resemble epileptic seizures. Her eyes roll back and she shakes so violently that she appears to be undergoing demonic possession. Another vixen named Alicia Klass loves anal sex, and talks about how wonderful it feels the entire time she's participating in it on camera.

At the end of her time in adult films, Christi Lake is certain to be remembered most for her Fann Fuxx series. In these tapes, which currently number seven, she has sex with selected fans who have written to her and sent a picture of themselves requesting that they be in one of her videos.

Christi then stars in, directs, and markets the videos through her Christilake.com website, or sells them to a larger distributor for a lump sum, maintaining the right to use clips from them on the Internet.

The series was conceptualized in 1995, when Christi was receiving a lot of mail from fans that had seen her early work. Many wanted to know about her swinging lifestyle, where they might meet her or hook up with her. Others asked if they could hire her as an escort, or inquired how they might get into the business. Then a friend of Christi's, who uses the name N. Smith and operates a website called creampie.com, suggested that she start a website to help market her talents and peripheral businesses. Her current website is well organized and sophisticated and plays off the Las Vegas-based Area

51 theme of extraterrestrials. When the homepage first comes on a spaceman with a cone of light magically makes Christi's clothes disappear. As adult websites go, it's certainly one of the most creative.

"N. Smith designed the site and put it on the web for me before I even understood what the Web was," Christi says. "So after getting all this fan mail I thought, What should I do next? I was not interested in prostitution or escort work, because it's illegal in Las Vegas, and since I have relatives in law enforcement I didn't particularly want to get busted."

> *One applicant who was accepted had a very simple reason for wanting to appear in Fann Fuxx — revenge.*

Christi clearly understood the allure of making adult films to some people in the outside world, so she and John bought their own video camera and presented an opportunity for Joe Lunchbucket to be a porn star for a day. The rules for the public were simple: send in a clothed photograph and in 100 words or less explain why you want to be in a sex film with Christi Lake. Anyone sending in a nude photo had it shredded. "I didn't want to see the goodies," says Christi. "What I was looking for was personality and charisma. Of course, it helped if they were hot looking."

In the beginning, she received 20 to 30 requests a week, but once the series was launched the volume increased significantly.

One applicant who was accepted had a very simple reason for wanting to appear in Fann Fuxx. He wrote that he'd recently been in a relationship that ended badly and he wanted to get revenge on his girlfriend. "I thought that sounded like a very good reason," Christi says, "so I selected him."

For the work, which takes a full day or two and for which the actor or actress is paid $100, a release must be signed allowing the film to be distributed worldwide and on the Internet. So an applicant has to at least give serious consideration to the consequences of fulfilling his or her particular fantasy.

The selected fan can describe what he'd like to do on camera, and unless it's exceptionally bizarre or kinky, it will be worked into the video. "They always tell me afterwards that it was harder than they thought it would be," Christi says, "because once you're having hot sex it's never a lot of fun to stop the camera and rearrange the lighting and change film."

I ask what happens when a guy gets so excited that he has an orgasm about two minutes into the shoot? -

"Oh, that happens," she says, "but that's the beauty of editing. You just move that to the end of the scene. I always recommend to the men that they not have any sexual relations or masturbate for at least three days before I arrive in their town. Of course, they don't always listen. One guy admitted that he masturbated just before he left his house for the shoot and therefore he couldn't come when we were shooting the video. I ended up using the scene in a montage of all the failed scenes, sort of a sex bloopers reel."

On a visit to a sociology class at UNLV in the late spring of 2003, Christi addresses a class of 25 students for over two hours, explaining every aspect of her career and facing all questions, no matter how difficult or critical, without blinking. Prior to her talk, she had requested of the course instructor, Dr. Barbara Brents, that the students turn in on paper their off-hand impressions of a woman who makes adult movies. Here is a sampling of responses:

— "I think that prostitution is degrading to women. They are looked at as pieces of meat. I have seen only one porn film in my life and it was nothing but women sucking, swallowing, and other horrible things. I believe the women who make these films are whores."

— "Women in pornography are nasty and slutty with big boobs. They meet the demands of men any time. They will do anything the director says, even if it goes against their morals."

— "How can people make these movies knowing their faces are going to be seen by millions of people? Is everyone who does these films doing it willingly? What about their families? What do their parents or husbands think?"

> *"The act of a woman taking money directly for sex is simply a one-to-one transaction for gratification, while what I do is art."*
>
> –Christi Lake

In Christi's lecture she begins by telling the personal story she has shared with me, plus information about how large the adult film industry has become. She tells the class that 8,000 adult videos are released every year, and that four major companies, VCA, Vivid, Extreme, and Wicked are the 800-pound gorillas of the industry.

She defends her occupation as being much different than prostitution. She says, "The act of a woman taking money directly for sex is simply a one-to-one transaction for gratification, while what I do is art, performing in such a way as to get the audience en masse excited and help them enjoy great sex, whether as a couple or alone."

She opines that most of the A-list talent in Hollywood watches adult films but says that, "They love to hate us. I would bet you Julia Roberts, who hears from people all the time how wonderful she is, watches our films in her private life. But people are probably not going to come up to me on the street and say, 'I loved your performance in Anal Gang Bang.'"

This last line gets a big laugh from the class, which warms up to her about 10 minutes into her talk.

Christi also tells the students that she dislikes the term pornography, "because the minute the word is mentioned people think of child pornography, or crimes against children. I can tell you without question that we don't want kids viewing our stuff and we certainly don't want them in our business."

She cites the case of Traci Lords, who got the entire industry in trouble when it was discovered in the late 1980s that she had lied about her age and appeared in dozens of sex films before she turned 18. "The irony is that once she was busted, she claimed she was forced into it, and drugged, and all these things. Several companies got in big trouble, but nothing happened to her. And because she portrayed herself as a victim, she was even forgiven by Hollywood and went on to a reasonable career in mainstream film and television work."

(In a summer interview with VEGAS magazine, Lords disputes the notion that being at the center of a scandal in the adult industry helped her mainstream career in any way. She told interviewer Stephen Saban, "Trying to start a legitimate acting career with a porn star past was like launching from a rotted pier, like building a house on quicksand . . . . You know, everybody's gonna have their opinion on that . . . and my opinion is that it hurt me much more than it ever helped me.")

At the end of the UNLV classroom visit, which runs 30 minutes over the allotted time without a single student leaving, Christi asks the class to write a short after-the-fact assessment of what they now think of her and her profession. Here are a few of those responses:

— "I feel that this is a legitimate profession, no different or more degrading than any other profession."

— "I have a different view totally of your profession. You are a down to earth person. To be honest, I want to get a video with you in it."

— "You've made me open my mind a bit. I might watch a film. I do think you're probably an exception to the industry being that you're very articulate. Women I've seen in television interviews have portrayed the industry as evil."

As she gathers up her notes and prepares to leave, Christi is surrounded by students requesting autographed pictures, which she happily signs with personal notes. As many female students as males make this request. Christi then presents to Dr. Brents her Christi Lake Decathlete vibrator, a 10-speed model which she designed herself. Dr. Brents is amused and slightly embarrassed by the unexpected gesture, but she graciously thanks Christi and asks her to return soon for another presentation.

Christi knows her time is running out as an adult actress, but she has no plans for leaving Las Vegas. Rather, she and John have been working for two years on an exit strategy that has them owning and operating their own small business. "It won't be operating off the Christi Lake name," she says. "But if someone comes in and does business with us because they know who I am and wants to visit with me, that's fine."

Christi says she has always loved Las Vegas for similar reasons as other adult performers who move here. "I'm one hour from L.A. by plane to make films that are shot there, and it's kind of a crossroads for people in our industry. All your friends come through here a couple of times a year, so you don't have to leave to see people you care about. And the home prices here are so much better than California. My house is the best investment I've got. And hey, we're Sin City here.

"Yes, I miss Minnesota with all the lakes and trees and beautiful country," she says. "But Sin City is the place for a person like me."

How Mainstream is Porn?

While Ashlyn Gere makes an annual income in the low six figures as an A-list star in the adult film business (by comparison Julia Roberts make $20 million per movie from mainstream Hollywood), the really big bucks are being split up among the producers, distributors, and cable providers who quietly make her films available to an ever-increasing consumer audience.

The New York Times estimated in a 2001 article by Frank Rich titled "Naked Capitalists," that Americans spend $4 billion a year on video pornography, and that when you add in porn networks, pay-per-view movies on cable and satellite, internet web sites and phone sex, the total exceeds $10 billion. That figure makes pornography a bigger entertainment business than major league baseball, the National Football League, and the NBA combined. "People pay more money for pornography in America in a year than they do on movie tickets, more than they do on all the performing arts combined," Rich writes.

Wall Street's Dennis McAlpine, an entertainment industry analyst for over two decades for the investment banking firm Auerbach, Pollak and Richardson, concurred with the $10 billion figure in an August, 2001, interview with the producers of the PBS series *Frontline*. McAlpine says it's hard to put an accurate number on a business that intentionally tries to keep its numbers down so as not to draw too much attention from the government, but he says that with pay-on-demand video in millions of American homes, adult film rentals available with the press of a button in most business hotels, and the growth of the Internet, the audience for adult movies has never been bigger and is growing by a large percentage each year.

McAlpine estimates that AT&T Broadband, with approximately 10 million subscribers, can earn up to $15 or $20 million a month if 10 percent of their subscribers pay for one adult film per month. That conservative estimate would generate over $200 million annually for AT&T, without the company's having to pay any production costs for movies that are supplied to them by distributors.

So the question is raised: Is a mainstream, conventional powerhouse like AT&T in the pornography business? The response that *Frontline's* producers got from an AT&T spokesman after repeated attempts was vague. "We don't talk about adult fare because we don't want to advertise it," the spokesman said. "We think if the public wants it, we'll give it to them. But we don't go out and advertise and try to sell it, because we don't think that's right."

McAlpine says, "They just don't want to get the city councilman upset and then breathing down their necks. So they say, 'We're just doing it because we have to. It's freedom of speech. We can't control what's on the program.'"

McAlpine attributes the increasing popularity of renting adult fare at home or in hotels to a sense of privacy that wasn't available before. "The consumer is now given a way of getting home video without going to the store and walking out with a brown paper bag with a title that he's afraid his next-door neighbor is going to see," he says. "He's getting that video delivered directly to his home or his hotel room, and he thinks nobody knows he's got it."

"Is a mainstream, conventional powerhouse like AT&T in the pornography business?

In the year 2000, according to a survey conducted by Adult Video News, 11,000 new hardcore sex titles hit the American marketplace. By comparison, in 1990 there were only 800. Clearly, with the mainlining of pornography directly to the consumer, adult video dealers are enjoying a boom industry, and the market for pretty women like Ashlyn Gere and Christi Lake to get a small piece of the consumer dollar in adult fare is a long way from drying up.

Gidget Goes Porn

"*For you know, dear —
I may, without vanity, hint —
Though an angel should write,
still 'tis devils must print.*"

— THOMAS MOORE

She has the face of an angel, albeit one that might have been expelled from heaven for giving too many come-hither glances. In fact, she had been called "Angel Face" often enough, while frolicking in the sun of Southern California as a surfer girl, that when her looks and figure thrust her into a world where her name had to be changed to protect the innocent, she chose Angela Summers. It was the perfect stage name for a tanned and toned beach bunny with a Catholic school background.

Some 14 years after making her first adult film, and nine years since she gave it up in the interest of marriage and motherhood, Angela Summers seems completely untainted by the experience. Her marriage to a construction worker is happy and stable. They have two lovely young daughters together, and Angela is deeply involved in her children's lives and school activities. The family lives in an attractive home in northwest Las Vegas, and I can't help but notice on the day of our interview, just prior to Halloween, that their beautifully maintained residence has more pumpkins and ghosts and goblins decorating the front yard than any other in her neighborhood. Once again I'm reminded that porn queens can't be easily typed; this one is equal parts Martha Stewart and Marilyn Chambers.

It all started rather innocently for Angela. She'd had plenty of attention from the boys in her middle-American high school and was popular with girls as well, winning a coveted spot on the cheerleading squad. She describes her upbringing as conservative, but she was never burdened by the guilt issues often instilled by a Catholic school education. She wasn't the type to lie in bed at night and worry about the dissuasions of the nuns or the fires of hell. She says she really didn't receive any sex education at all from her teachers or parents.

"If they did tell us about the birds and bees, they did it very quickly and without much detail," she says, laughing. "It was just a topic that I guess they were uncomfortable with, so we had to explore it on our own. Of course, any time you make something taboo, it somehow becomes more appealing."

Angela says she nearly made it to high school graduation as a virgin, holding off the ultimate act until her senior year. It wasn't that she had moral reservations about sex, but rather because "no one had ever tried." Maybe the boys were just intimidated, because her friends from that time describe her as "the best looking girl in the school." But once it happened, any reluctance she had about exploring the limits of her sexuality was stripped away as fast as her clothes.

"I loved sex right away," she says. "The first time I did it the boy didn't know I was a virgin, because I sure didn't tell him. But it felt very natural. I'd never actually seen people having sex in a movie or in magazines, and I'd never been exposed to anyone doing it, but it didn't require much practice to know exactly how it was done. I was able to climax right away, and I couldn't get enough. I guess I was just born horny because I was always in the mood. And the idea of being totally faithful to one boyfriend never made a lot of sense to me. I was in an open relationship with a guy when I was first drawn to the adult-film business."

Angela's long-time friend Sue, who moved to Las Vegas last year from Florida to accept a management position with a food distribution company, remembers the day they met, in 10th grade. "I was driving to school with my brother and he pulled next to this car with a beautiful girl in it," she says. "Of course, he tried to hit on her." She describes a scene right out of *American Graffiti*, where the Richard

Dreyfuss character spots his dream girl (Suzanne Somers) at a stop-light and is instantly infatuated.

"All the boys loved Angela," Sue says. "But when I got to know her and she became my best friend, I had no reason to be jealous. She was sweet and popular and it gave me a certain status to be friends with such an adorable and popular girl. And we discovered that we had the exact same birthday, and a lot of the same interests, so our friendship happened very naturally."

Sue says that both she and Angela were "pretty wild" in high school, and affirms that once her friend discovered sex, there was no turning back. "Angela definitely loved sex and all the attention," she says. "And even though she was a free spirit, she always managed to keep her head on straight. She didn't get into the drug thing like some of our friends. Oh, there was a little drinking at parties, but she always had a pretty good grip on who she was and what she wanted from life."

Two years after graduating from high school and working as a temp secretary for seven dollars an hour, Angela, on a lark, decided with another girlfriend to answer an ad in an underground newspaper. She interviewed for a job with a phone sex company, where customers would pay exorbitant fees to breathy voiced "actresses" pretending to be interested in them. It didn't sound difficult. All she'd have to do was engage in suggestive word play, get the guy off, bill his credit card, and take the next call.

"I was looking for something I could do in the evening at home for about ten bucks an hour, just for extra spending money," she says.

"But when I went in for the interview and to fill out an application, the man said, 'Oh, with your looks you shouldn't be doing phone calls. You should be modeling for the print ads and posters for this company.'"

Angela was asked to pose for some bikini stills that would be used to market the 900 number. She was paid three hundred dollars for a one-hour photo shoot, which was more money than she'd made the previous week as a secretary working a full 40 hours.

"And it was a whole lot more fun," she says. "The pictures looked good and everyone made a fuss over them. I realized very quickly that I was an exhibitionist. My life as a secretary ended that day."

Shortly after her modeling debut, Angela was asked to attend an audition for potential adult film actresses. The session was held at Jim South's World Modeling, which is the gateway for the majority of young women who become porn stars, including Ashlyn Gere and Christi Lake. Again, she had no reservations about taking what many would consider a daunting leap. An audition usually does not involve actual sex, but does involve getting naked in front of strangers. But Angela found no discomfort at all in doing that, and thought the audition "went great. I had worked out my whole life and was proud of my body," she says. "I was totally uninhibited."

Her first film was called *Wild Goose Chase*, and it was directed by John Stagliano, known in the adult biz as "The Buttman. "

"John is totally into bubble butts," explains Angela, "and I have one."

For about eight hours of work on her first video and one long sex scene with a veteran actor, Joey Silvera, Angela was paid $2,000. Her good looks also landed her on the box cover of the movie, which in adult films made her an "A" girl. That meant her face and body were appealing enough to sell the film or enhance its rental ability at video stores.

"I remember John almost apologizing when he gave me the check," she says. "He asked, 'Are you sure this is enough money?'

"And I thought to myself, 'Are you kidding?' It was the biggest check I'd ever received. It was so much fun I would have done it for free."

When I remark that her attitude about sex was more like that of a carefree young man, she agrees. "I think that's accurate," she says. "If you tell a typical young guy he can have sex with lots of beautiful women and get paid for it, he's not going to have to think too hard to decide that's a good deal. That's the way I was. It was like, 'Where do I sign up?'"

> "And I thought to myself, 'Are you kidding?' It was the biggest check I'd ever received."
>
> — ANGELA SUMMERS

"Not even a moment's hesitation about the implications of having sex on film?" I inquire, starting to feel prudish that I'm even asking the question.

"Absolutely not," she replies. "I found the whole thing a total turn-on. It was like acting out all the sexual fantasies I'd had as a teenager. But I didn't think for a minute that this would start a career of doing movies. I thought it was more of a lark, a one-time deal, and then I immediately started getting all these calls for more work."

Later that year, *Wild Goose Chase* swept several awards at the Adult Video News Awards, including the Best Film of the Year 1991, and Angela was honored as New Starlet of the Year.

Chapter 4

"I was actually involved with John Stagliano when I did that first movie," she says. "He's the only man in the business I ever had a relationship with. But it was great because he flew me all over the world. We went to South America and Europe where we shot a bunch of two- and three-day movies, often employing amateur talent in gonzo (unscripted and semi-spontaneous) situations. There was one movie where we picked these two brothers up right off the beach, and I had sex with them in a hotel room. They thought they'd died and gone to heaven."

Angela made about 15 to 20 films her first year in the business and quickly became known as a hot commodity. Success in her industry happened virtually overnight for a girl who prior to her first appearance in a sex film had never even seen one.

"I was this little Catholic girl who had never been exposed to sex in any way," she says. "And now it was my full-time career. But it didn't scare me in the least. I found it all very exciting and liberating. I suppose you could say I was naïve to all the dangers of sexually transmitted diseases, but I never caught anything. Don't ask me why. Just lucky, I guess."

> *"There was one movie where we picked these two brothers up right off the beach and I had sex with them in a hotel room. They thought they'd died and gone to heaven."*
>
> —ANGELA SUMMERS

She shares an unpleasant story about one close call with a sexually transmitted disease.

"I was doing a photo shoot with two guys in the business, just some still pictures to promote a movie," she says. "And I noticed something moving on one of the guys, near his crotch. Now being a nice person,

I didn't scream or embarrass him on the set. I just whispered in his ear that we needed to step into the other room. I asked him to look down at his crotch, and you've never seen such a zoo. There were about half a dozen crabs crawling around on him. It was the grossest thing you've ever seen. He freaked out and went home, of course. And our makeup artist went to the drug store, and the other actor and I showered in some blue chemical medicine, just in case one had jumped on us. Then they washed and vacuumed the couch we were posing on, and I had to redo my hair and makeup. It was just one of those long horrible days you don't forget."

What Angela wouldn't fully appreciate until she'd been in the business a while was that she was the complete package that adult film producers are looking for: a great looking girl with a hot body who absolutely loves sex and is willing to reveal it on camera. If the girl can also act and is good with dialogue, like an Ashlyn Gere, so much the better, but that's not a requirement. Nothing is less important to pornophiles than a great plot.

I recall a friend of mine, an avid porn watcher, saying that the movie *Deep Throat*, which many movie critics credit as launching adult films into a mainstream-viewing trend in the 1970s, had ruined sex films for him.

"Because *Deep Throat* employed humor so much, and relied on a laugh track," he says, "it seemed every porn film for the next five years used a gimmick or comic device to try to inject humor into the story. We don't watch fuck films to get a laugh," he says. "I mean, c'mon!"

Chapter 4

Similarly, pornophiles aren't interested in sophisticated story lines or great romance either. If a man's looking for those he can always rent *The Godfather* trilogy or *Dr. Zhivago*. When he watches a sex film, it's to get quickly turned on and get his jollies, and then switch to SportsCenter. Statistics from the Las Vegas based Hospitality Network, which owns the rights to hotel room movie rentals in Southern Nevada, reveal that the average amount of time that hotel guests spend watching adult films — for which they pay up to thirteen dollars plus tax — is seven minutes. Needless to say, character development and the intricacies of story line are instantly negated once a viewer achieves orgasm. Or should we just say that in an adult film, the climax and the ending are the same thing.

While there is a niche in the adult industry for couples films where romance is part of the equation, they occupy just a small segment of the market. Most of the couples films which often show on the Playboy Channel are directed by females who used to be into hardcore porn, and are tired of women in adult films being portrayed solely as sexual victims. Couples films employ softer lighting, show more kissing and intimacy and foreplay, and totally avoid gangbangs, anal sex, and facial cumshots.

> *The average amount of time that hotel guests spend watching adult films is seven minutes.*

While Angela calls herself a totally uninhibited free spirit, she had boundaries about what she would and wouldn't do on film.

"I didn't do interracial movies because I'm not attracted to other races," she says. "And I didn't do anal because that's not enjoyable to me. Why would I do something that hurts? I was doing these films because they were exciting to me and pleasurable, and if it didn't seem like a movie was going to be a lot of fun I would take a pass on it."

Angela's friend Sue recalls how she learned about her friend's adult career. "She told me she had something to tell me when I was visiting her one time," she says. "And I could tell she was sort of nervous about breaking the news. But once she got it out, I can't say I was surprised. I always knew she loved sex and craved attention and liked making money, so in that sense the business gave her all three. I also knew that, whatever career she chose, she would treat it like a business and would hang onto her money because she's very frugal. You might even call her a cheapskate. She loves to shop garage sales, if you can believe it."

Less than two years into the adult film business, Angela was asked by the Lee Agency, one of the top strip club dance agencies, if she wanted to become a featured dancer on the road. Again, she was invited into a world she knew little about. She had never been to one of these clubs, but she had heard of other adult headliners who were making more money dancing than by doing videos.

"I said I'd try it," she says, "so I made this homemade costume, with an ultra-feminine little white skirt and wings and a halo. My persona was Angela, the little angel."

The Century Theatre in San Francisco put her name on its marquee under the billing, Adult Starlet of the Year, Angela Summers, and although she was extremely nervous when her routine started, she says it quickly went away.

"I saw the excitement on the men's faces and I got really into it," she recalls. "I realized that like the films, this was something that would be fun and that I'd be able to handle it."

Angela had two breast enhancements in the early 90s, after her dancing career started and before her adult film career ended. "I could see that to really make great money as a headliner on the dance-tour circuit, I needed bigger and better boobs," she says. "So I got them."

And she soon found that the money from dancing was even better than making films. "They paid me $5000 for the week, plus I could earn a ton more money off of stuff like Polaroids ($20 apiece to sit topless on a customer's lap; the film costs her 84 cents per print), and selling autographed pictures, sexual souvenirs, and even the underwear she wore into the place. She found that customers who are infatuated with a dancer will do almost anything to impress her or make personal contact with her.

"I can buy panties at the 99-cent store and sell them for $15 each," she says. "But there are guys who've had a few drinks who've dropped hundred-dollar bills on the table for a pair of panties. It's crazy sometimes."

> *"I can buy panties at the 99-cent store and sell them for $15 each."*
>
> –ANGELA SUMMERS

Angela's initial concerns about security on the dance circuit were eased when she learned that every club where she would be performing would provide a bodyguard and an assistant for the week. And there were other star treatment amenities as well.

"I am always put up in a nice hotel, and taken good care of," she says. "The agencies and clubs know they can't keep good girls working on the dance circuit unless they treat them well. If a girl is mistreated in any way, the word will spread quickly and the club will lose all its girls."

Unlike the majority of girls who enter the porn world, Angela had an appreciation for the value of a dollar, and she had heard too many tales about other adult actresses who had made good money for a year or two and blown it all on drugs or the fast life.

"I was never into drugs, and I didn't spend money on clothes or boyfriends," she says. "I put my money in mutual funds at a time when the stock market was on the rise, and I did pretty well."

Another long-time friend of Angela's named Timi, who met her when they waitressed at the same restaurant in the San Fernando Valley, says that her friend goes beyond frugal. "I think it's fair to say she's a real tight-ass," she says, and then laughs when she realizes the double entendre. "But maybe that's why she was so popular in porn."

Timi says that Angela has maintained a relatively normal, adjusted life through her career choices "because she had a loving family that was close." Timi has reason to know about the family bonds, as she recently married Angela's oldest brother Thomas, thereby becoming her sister-in-law. "She's always felt like a sister to me," she says with a laugh. "When we first became friends I was into bodybuilding and was pretty strong, and I always felt like her bodyguard when we'd go clubbing because all the guys were always hitting on her."

Unlike Angela's friend Sue, who says watching Angela's films would make her uncomfortable, Timi says she's seen several of her movies, and, "They make me hot. She's great in them. It's also fun to watch some of her early films because I spot articles of my clothing in them — dresses and blouses she borrowed from me."

After three years in adult films, Angela was living in a rented beach house in Los Angeles, but she was looking for a better investment. She'd heard that land values and home prices were reasonable in Las Vegas, so she rented an apartment near the Strip and hired a realtor to take her around town to look at houses. She eventually bought a new home in Summerlin in 1994.

She also met a man in her apartment complex who worked construction, and they clicked immediately. Always upfront and honest, Angela told him on their first date how she made her living. She hadn't made a film in a few months, and was actually contemplating retiring from the industry because of recent news that a few better-known performers had tested HIV-positive. As their romance blossomed, and they got married and planned a family, Angela knew she wouldn't go back to making films.

"There was just no need at that point to continue with the movies," she says. "I had enjoyed it and have absolutely no regrets about any of it, but I had moved to a different place in my life at that point. But I also wanted to keep dancing because I enjoyed it, and it is a good source of income."

Since her first dancing gig in the early 90s, Angela says the money has now doubled, and some top adult stars have even broken into the $25,000 per week range. "There's such an underground market and following of porn stars," she says. "You don't fully appreciate it until you meet some of these people, and they tell you they've seen all your films and that they check out your website on a regular basis."

It seems to matter not at all to her many fans that Angela hasn't made a XXX film in nearly a decade. They have remained loyal, and she still gets booked for one dancing gig a month, on the average.

"Angela made a ton of films during the years she was working, and through that developed a large fan base," says Tony Indovino, owner of the Lee Network, which represents 90 percent of the adult film stars who double as feature dancers. His client list includes adult superstars like Ginger Lynn, Amber Lynn, Ashlyn Gere, and Jenna Jameson.

"An actress who made a large impact, like Angela, and who is a good dancer and popular personality, can keep a following for years and do well," he says. "You could say that she is the exception and not the rule, but good for her."

Angela also makes occasional appearances at adult video conventions, but usually in the role of interviewer for adult news channels or compilation tapes. A glib and perky conversationalist, she's good at getting the quick sound bite and asking the direct questions that adult fans are interesting in hearing.

During the week of the Adult Video News Awards in January, 2003, Angela was given a Legends of the Adult Industry Award, which was presented to her by John Stagliano. A good crowd turned out for the ceremony, and Angela indulged them by baring her trademark posterior. They responded with a standing ovation.

She is surprised and sad about the news that her friend Stagliano tested HIV positive. She says he told her he got it from a hooker in Brazil, after having anal sex and then realizing it was a man in drag. "It's kind of a hard story to comprehend," she says. "But the facts don't matter as much as the sad news that he's infected. John is really a nice guy, and he was greatly responsible for my success in adult films."

As I prepare to leave, she tells me her only concern about her film career is that it could in the future be a hindrance to her daughters. "I worry that years from now my daughters might want to go to law school or med school or maybe run for political office and someone would dig up something about me, and it would count against them," she says. "Maybe I'm just paranoid, like any mother, but that would be the only thing that would give me a regret about my career."

Schwing! The Etiquette of Mate Swapping

"He had wooed one by one each of the half-dozen women who were now part of his circle, and by sharing his wife with the men, and creating a permission-giving atmosphere that fostered open sexuality within the group, he believed that he was forming the nucleus of a cult that would soon appeal to many other couples who truly believed in coequal relationships."

— Gay Talese, *Thy Neighbor's Wife*

W hat image comes to mind when you think of swingers? Could it be the "wild and crazy guys" played by Dan Ackroyd and Steve Martin on Saturday Night Live, with their Scotch plaid bell-bottoms and paisley shirts open to the navel? Or do you picture a dumpy middle-aged couple who leave their home several nights a month with bowling-ball bags and a twinkle in their eyes?

When you add Las Vegas to the equation, perhaps the stereotype would be of the aging showgirl and the sloe-eyed blackjack dealer, both a tad weary of each other and looking to ratchet up the excitement quotient under a neon moon.

One sure way to see what actual Las Vegas swingers look like is to log onto vegasredrooster.com and visit the website of Mike and Chris Borchers, who have hosted swinging parties at their ranch-style house off Boulder Highway since 1982. The home-page portrait of the couple, which is several years old, looks like a formal portrait taken for the annual installment dinner of the Moose Lodge, or one of those J.C. Penney one-hour specials you purchase as an heirloom before Grandpa has the big one. While the Borchers are certainly a pleasant-looking couple who by all published and word-of-mouth accounts make fine hosts, their photo doesn't exactly send blood rushing to the erogenous zones. Nor for that matter do any of the other photos on the Red Rooster site, including the so-called "Nasty Girl parties." You discover as you browse that Las Vegas swingers are just average looking people who share a few things in common: i.e. they like to get naked and are more than willing to have sex with people they've met just moments before.

One Red Rooster patron named Laura even has her own website that is bannered on the home page, and she is happy to tell you everything about herself. She offers dozens of nude photos for your

Chapter 5

viewing pleasure. Laura reveals that she's about 40, was born in Las Vegas, has lived here her entire life, has completed the task of raising her children, and that she and her partner Lee just love to swing. Laura's site even tells you all of her sexual preferences.

"I love oral sex," she writes, "both giving and receiving, (and yes, I swallow.)"

For some casual browsers, this may be a little more information than they require, but then casual browsers don't usually spend much time on sites that offer Adults-Only warnings. Those who give in to curiosity quickly learn that they are but a single finger click away from having their eye poked out by a throbbing penis, or the vision of a woman spreading her legs so wide the viewer feels like he's preparing to do a pap smear.

> *"I love oral sex," she writes, "both giving and receiving, (and yes, I swallow.)"*
>
> —LAURA

An abbreviated history of wife swapping in the United States might include the following highlights:

According to the *Illustrated Book of Sexual Records* — a must-have for anyone concerned with such factoids as the most recorded orgasms in one hour, or the shortest man ever to have sex on film with the tallest woman (and how they did it) — the first magazine article devoted solely to the topic of wife swapping in America appeared in 1957.

A New York men's magazine called *Mr.* carried a short article on the subject, and included a sidebar "correspondence section," which gave the phone numbers of men willing to share their wives sexually with others so inclined. Today, thousands of tabloids and small magazines around the country, including several in Las Vegas, publish contact information about couples willing to participate in consensual extramarital relationships.

Clubs like the Red Rooster Too in Commercial Center on West Sahara Avenue, and the Green Door, at a nearby location, actively solicit swinging couples — and single ladies — through their websites, and in *The Mercury*, a weekly Las Vegas tabloid. A July 2003 visit to the Green Door website announced the opening of a new adult social club called Illusions. While these clubs seem to come and go with the seasons, there is strong suspicion that they are not true swingers' clubs — in the sense that married couples or partners go there to swap mates — but rather fronts for prostitution. KLAS TV8 investigative reporter George Knapp discovered through an undercover operation in early 2003 that a network of local cab drivers and limousine drivers all knew that the Las Vegas social clubs catered to single men. Several drivers who were asked about the prostitution operations in Pahrump advised the men inquiring that they could get everything at these clubs that was available in Pahrump, without the long drive. A local limousine driver named William confirmed for me in an interview that there's an ongoing sweetheart arrangement with these new-age swing clubs that any driver delivering a customer to the club will get the full $45 cover charge kicked back to him.

"A single guy can get anything he wants in those places," William said. "And there's no risk at all for us drivers. We're just recommending a place and taking a customer where he wants to go."

One club called Hot Bodies Spa promises to reward even more than a full admission-fee kickback. In the March 2003 local edition of *Taxi & Limo Drivers' Guide*, the club announces, "We are Very Driver Friendly. The customer pays $40 and the Driver gets $60 cash back. Nobody pays more!"

Obviously, somebody is paying more, and it happens to be the unsuspecting customer whose rationale and common sense go out the window when he's lured by the prospect of wild sex with a stranger.

Swinging took a big leap into the pop-culture lexicon in 1969 when the film *Bob & Carol & Ted & Alice* packed theaters and got everyone talking. The movie tells the story of a documentary filmmaker named Bob, played by Robert Culp, and his wife Carol, played by Natalie Wood, who go to a remote California retreat for group therapy. While there the couple gets caught up in the Age of Aquarius and the anything-goes atmosphere of the Woodstock generation, and before long Bob and Carol are home preaching radical new ideas about open marriage and free love to their best friends Ted and Alice (Elliot Gould and Dyan Cannon). The two couples are soon headed to Las Vegas to put their new openness to a test. The result is a ménage-a-quatre which became great fodder for late-night talk shows and raised several issues for the average American married couple.

B&C&T&A was a commercial success for several reasons, not the least of which was the sex appeal of the two actresses. Dyan Cannon and Natalie Wood in panties and bras fueled the fantasies of most mainstream American men. It got men wondering: What would it be like to sleep with the good-looking wives of their friends and get away with it?

Then in 1973 New York Yankee baseball pitchers Fritz Peterson and Mike Kekich participated in the most publicized trade of that season. They swapped wives. Newspaper and magazine articles about Mike and Suzanne and Fritz and Marilyn popped up everywhere.

In New York a swing club called Plato's Retreat began to flourish by the late 1970s, around the same time that the movie *Saturday Night Fever* and the exclusive nightclub Studio 54 were all the rage. Plato's received immense national publicity as a place where couples could go and have open sex with strangers by the hour. A Las Vegas photographer, Robert Scott Hooper, and his assistant Theresa Holmes, were commissioned by *Playboy* magazine to shoot a pictorial at Plato's Retreat. The resulting feature, which showed attractive young people rollicking nude through hot tubs and saunas and indulging their every carnal desire, made the club a national sensation.

> *The sexual revolution was in full swing, and there didn't seem to be much of a downside.*

Hooper told me shortly after the pictorial appeared that dozens of great-looking women regularly patronized Plato's Retreat, and men from age 20 to 60 told him they frequented the club as often as three or four times a week. The sexual revolution was in full swing, and there didn't seem to be much of a downside.

Then in 1980 respected journalist Gay Talese, whose resume included books like *The Kingdom and the Power* about the *New York Times*, and *Honor Thy Father*, chronicling the rise of the Mafia in America, completed a nine-year study on the sexual revolution and changing morals in the U.S. His book, *Thy Neighbor's Wife*, soared to the top of the bestseller lists.

Chapter 5

In the book, Talese boldly (or perhaps recklessly) admitted to many extramarital affairs. As research, he worked at two different New York massage parlors, and he spent weeks at the Sandstone Retreat at Big Sur, a commune that encouraged open marriage and promoted sexual freedom. Over 100 pages of *Thy Neighbor's Wife* detail and celebrate the lifestyle of *Playboy* publisher Hugh Hefner. Talese's study represented another credible endorsement for open sexuality. The author's wife Nan Talese, then a prominent book editor at Simon & Schuster, not surprisingly separated from him during this period, claiming that his research was an irreparable detriment to their marriage.

For sexual libertarians and swingers, the years from 1967 to about 1982 marked a golden era. And then the AIDS virus seeped into the public consciousness and started claiming lives among those who didn't practice safe sex, in both the gay and heterosexual population. The mysterious new disease threw a wet blanket over the burning coals of unrestricted sexual passion.

Because they were profiled and openly discussed their lifestyle on two segments of HBO's popular "Real Sex" series, Las Vegas residents Hank Armstrong and his wife Anna Malle are among the best-known swinging couples in the country. Since the HBO stories ran in 1996 and '97, Hank and Anna have become a poster couple for the swinging lifestyle, and when they attend Lifestyles conventions (the most popular swinging gatherings in the country), they are treated almost like celebrities. If Anna's name is familiar, it is because she is also an adult film actress and national touring feature dancer with her own fan club and website.

Hank and Anna met about 14 years ago in Fort Myers, Florida. Hank was a bartender in a topless club called the Foxy Lady Lounge, which was owned by his brother. Anna, then working under a different name, was one of the club dancers. Hank had previously lived in Las Vegas and worked at local hot spots like Botany's and the Shark Club.

"I had heard about this good looking guy that was coming to work at our club, and that he was from Las Vegas, and I figured he'd come in here with this real big attitude," Anna says. "And I even told him that when I met him. But we became friends right away."

It's a warm summer day in Las Vegas and as we visit in the living room of their comfortable home in the southeast part of the city, Hank and Anna recount for me how they got together. They both are wearing t-shirts and shorts, and Anna's long brown legs reveal her years as a dancer. Her jet-black hair and exotic features suggest Indian blood, but she says she's a mix of several nationalities. Within minutes of the start of our conversation she makes a joke about her ample breasts, and how she had to save money for the implants that she felt were essential to both her movie and dancing careers.

"When we came to Las Vegas in 1991 to explore getting into the adult business, it was obvious that I was going to have to get a boob job to work in the industry," she says. "In Florida, nearly all the girls were natural, but here most of the dancers and adult actresses have implants. So I did what I had to do."

Did they become a couple right away? I inquire.

"No, it started with a lot of sex, with several girls from the club and couples and wild parties," Anna says. "We were two people who

Chapter 5

enjoyed fucking each other and oops, we fell in love. The relationship just kind of happened, and from the beginning we were cool with each other having sex with different people."

"What happened is I used to take the girls on weekends to out-call parties," Hank says. "Usually, people would phone up the club and ask for girls to come do a girl-girl show for a bachelor-party type situation. I would drive the girls to and from the party and make sure nothing funny happened, and I'd collect the money.

"There wasn't any sex happening at these deals," he says, "but the girls would get so worked up doing the party that on the way home we ended up fucking. I think you'd call that a good job for a horny guy."

"He was very good at what he was do-ing and the word got out and soon all the girls at the club wanted to do these bach-elor parties," Anna says. "Hank is very well endowed, and he was really toned up back then."

> *"We were two people who enjoyed fucking each other and oops, we fell in love."*
>
> —ANNA MALLE

Hank pats his stomach almost apolo-getically, acknowledging that the last 10 years have taken a slight toll on his physique.

As Hank and Anna's relationship grew and they became a couple, it was understood between them that they would continue to have an open relationship and seek out other partners. But Anna is quick to admit that jealousy was — and still is — an issue for her.

"When we decided to move out to Vegas and pursue the adult entertainment business, Hank would occasionally make comments about old girlfriends that lived here, and I can't deny that it bothered me," she says. "I was this little girl from Iowa who had found my way to Fort Myers, which is also a small town. And I was coming to a big city for the first time, so there were things that hit me in the pit of the stomach. It took me about two years before I was really comfortable and secure enough that he really loved me and that we were going to stay together."

Their actual entrée to swinging in a somewhat organized group setting was in 1993 at a Lifestyles convention in San Diego. Anna recalls it vividly.

"When we checked in at the hotel, there were about 50 people hanging around the registration area and there was not one person under 30," she says. "They were all age 50 and over. We were thinking we really screwed up coming there, but you can't say it out loud. I just remember thinking, Oh my!"

> "*You're not supposed to flirt and smile because that's an open invitation that you want to get together.*"
>
> —HANK ARMSTRONG

"We learned the ground rules pretty quickly," Hank says. "You're not supposed to flirt and smile because that's an open invitation that you want to get together."

"Yeah, I learned that one the hard way," says Anna. "You can't smile at everyone or it hurts their feelings when you don't want to fuck them."

Hank says that the agenda usually includes a pool party during the day, with everyone hanging out in swimsuits and bikinis, and then a theme party at night where conventioneers dress up in period costumes.

"Once we went down to the pool there were a lot of younger women in bikinis and high heels, with their men, and I started to think this was going to be okay," Hank says. "It was like the older people knew to hang out with their own group. There wasn't much crossing of lines. As long as you didn't come on to people or act too friendly you were all right. We stuck with [porn star] Nina Hartley, who we knew from the adult business, and she kind of showed us the ropes that first year."

Of a thousand couples in attendance that year, Hank says that he was sexually attracted to about 30 percent of the women.

In a three-day convention, how many times would the two of you have sex? I wonder.

"Oh numerous times," Hank quickly replies.

"Let me tell you about his all-time record," Anna says. "This one year we threw a huge party, and our door was propped open in the hotel, which is an open invitation to come on in. We had two double beds and at the end of the night I picked up all the condoms that Hank had used. Then we took a poll the next morning of the women who'd fucked Hank the previous day and all but one raised her hand.

> *". . . at the end of the night I picked up all the condoms that Hank had used. . . . and I counted 30."*
>
> —ANNA MALLE

I'm not saying he came with all of them, but he changed condoms with each penetration and I counted 30."

I look at Hank with a mixture of shock and grudging respect. "Damn, you're an animal," I say. He just shrugs, with a Whaddaya gonna do? look on his face.

"That's how I got my stage name," Anna says. "After a night of wild sex, Hank said, 'You're an animal,' and we decided that Anna Malle was a pretty good name for adult movies."

And how many men were you with that night? I ask Anna.

"Three or four," she says. "But I was also with a lot of the women."

Anna says there are times she really prefers sex with a woman, because "a woman is soft and gentle and really knows how to satisfy another woman." She says she appreciates a woman's softness and sensuality during sex.

"But then there are other times I just really want to be fucked hard," she says. "And that's when I want a man."

On the HBO special, Anna looks straight into the camera and plays with her breasts. "We think we're a sexy couple," she says. "Don't you think I'm sexy? And my husband is a very horny man, so the first thing I pack when we come to a convention is this big bottle of lube, because no woman can stay wet all weekend."

I ask about the fear of AIDS, and what impact it has on the swinging lifestyle.

"Since we first got involved in swinging we've been condom only," says Anna. "We don't believe in unprotected sex. But unfortunately that's not the case with everyone. Some of the people are still from that era when HIV wasn't around, and they don't believe it will ever happen to them."

The biggest issue Hank and Anna faced, which comes as no surprise to someone outside the lifestyle, was the green monster. Especially on her part.

"I've always had a problem with low self-esteem," she says. "I've overcome a lot of it by performing in movies and onstage, where sometimes I have too much self-esteem. But those insecurities about our relationship really snuck in those first two years we were dating and I guess I wasn't totally secure about our relationship."

"We had a lot of conversations, and really had to work on communicating with each other," says Hank. "It's important when you're changing partners that you both like the couple and that each of you is satisfied that you're having a fun experience."

"It was like that a lot of the time in those first years," Anna chimes in. "Hank would be with this gorgeous girl and totally into it and I'm with Joe Schmo over here with his big gut that I'm not in the least attracted to. We finally had a long discussion about this issue and I told Hank, "You need to not be so wrapped up in all the pussy around and you need to look over at me when I'm having a hard time with somebody or some guy that I'm not interested in is putting his hands all over me. I told him that I was still supposed to be Number One in his life and to remember that I was still in the room and had my own needs.""

As Anna is talking her voice rises and my hunch observing them is that the jealousy issue is still something they must address on occasion. Even a totally open relationship has to have some boundaries.

I've had a question brewing since our conversation began and I finally ask it:

"What does it take for a couple to reach the point where they can clearly separate sex and love into two categories that don't overlap? It occurs to me that is what it takes for a swinging relationship to stay together."

"It's certainly not for everybody," says Anna. "It requires great communication and trust. But sex is sex and love is love and there's a huge difference between the two."

"The problem is that a lot of people are hypocritical," says Hank. "They either don't admit that they cheat on their partner, or they engage in milder forms of cheating, like going to a titty bar behind their wife's back or flirting with other people. There is a line there that they can't cross so they do other things to satisfy their sexual drives. So many married couples hide things from each other and build up problems and guilt, and they don't talk about it because talking about sex is uncomfortable or maybe it was taboo when they were growing up, and so it's an aspect of their lives that they have never talked about.

"Or maybe they just masturbate a lot thinking about someone else," he adds. "It could be a variety of different things."

(With that comment I can't help but recall a moment in the HBO Real Sex documentary featuring Hank and Anna. A man is telling a gathering at the swingers' convention that he has been studying orgasm in laboratory settings for years, and that the record for one man having orgasms masturbating in a one-hour period is 17. And that the record number of climaxes for a woman is 134. I admit to being more impressed with the man's total than the woman's, simply because there was no way he could fake it. I also recall thinking that they ought to keep that man locked up in the laboratory. He could be dangerous roaming free among the general population.)

> *The record for one man having orgasms masturbating in a one-hour period is 17.*

In fairness to all swingers out there, Hank and Anna are two of the more "active" participants in the Lifestyles scene. A more conservative branch of the group would be represented by a married couple named Steve and Allison, who live in California and have attended the last two annual Lifestyles conventions in Las Vegas.

"This might sound crazy to you," Steve says, "but if I decided for some reason that I wasn't into sex anymore, I would still go to these meetings because the best friends we've ever made have been people we've met through this organization. It just seems that you can strike up conversations more quickly, and because there's an openness to the whole group, you find that people will really listen to you and offer great feedback. Nobody really has a hidden agenda. You don't bump into people that are judgmental or who just opened a Baptist ministry."

Steve and Allison have five children, all of them from previous marriages, and none of the kids have a clue that their parents have chosen the swinging lifestyle. (It occurs to me that they're like the Brady Bunch, but with a slight twist, or maybe not. With the post-series revelations that Robert Reed was gay, and that Barry Williams, the actor who played Greg, was rumored to have gotten cozy with Florence Henderson, perhaps no twisting is necessary.)

"Most of us who have chosen this means of expression in our marriages will run like mice when the lights are turned on," Steve says. "We don't want anyone outside the group knowing what we are doing, not because we are ashamed of it, but because the general perception of swingers is that we all get in piles of naked bodies all the time. One time I ran into a principal at one of my children's schools and we were both extremely embarrassed," he says. "I thought I was going to have a heart attack when I saw him. But then you quickly realize that you're there for the same reason, so we kind of kidded each other and got over it.

"I can tell you that in the 12 years we've been going to conventions and parties, I've never once seen an orgy, nor have my wife or I ever engaged in anonymous sex with people we've met just minutes before," he adds.

When I express surprise at this, he says, "That's our agreement. When I was at the Lifestyles Convention at the Aladdin (in August 2003), I fooled around a little with two different women in the pool, but I did not have penetration sex with anyone other than my wife that weekend. Had Allison been more interested in either of these women, we might have pursued it further."

Steve also swears that since he's been married he's never had an affair outside the boundaries of the swing clubs. "Why would I?" he says. "That would defeat the honesty and openness we've chosen to share. I like the fact that we can be in a grocery store or out shopping and I'll notice an attractive woman and say, 'Wow, look at that gorgeous woman over there,' and my wife won't get offended. The average guy is going to get elbowed, or his wife is going to be hurt that he's lusting after her."

Steve agrees with Hank Armstrong that while sex between females is accepted and encouraged in the swinging lifestyle, gay sex between men is totally taboo.

"You just don't see homosexual men at these gatherings," he says. "It's considered too creepy, and none of the men in this lifestyle are looking for other men."

I question him about the implicit double standard, and how it would seem to counter the open sex philosophy of the group. "Every organization has its boundaries and its traditions," he says. "And I can tell you that while nearly all the women are bisexual, if they were suddenly single and looking for another life partner they would seek out a man. It's just a universal fact of life that nearly all men love to watch two women together, but I don't know many women who want to watch men together. That's just the way it is."

Steve says that jealousies never cease to exist, even in the most open of relationships. "This lifestyle will still keep you on your toes," he says, because most people want to hang onto their primary lovers. "You find that even though most of the people in it are just average looking, vanilla people, they keep themselves in far better shape than they would if they weren't going to be seen naked by others. Men know they'll look better at the pool, and increase their attractiveness if they keep their belly flat and stay toned. It's almost like when I got divorced and lost a lot of weight. I knew I was going to be out there looking for another partner, and once you're involved in the singles scene again you need to take better care of yourself."

Steve was even willing to poll several other couples who attended the Lifestyles Convention at the Aladdin, in part to demonstrate that your run-of-the-mill swingers are not voracious sexual animals. Of the 20 couples he contacted with a promise of anonymity, only one couple had sex with more than four couples in the four days of the convention. (That pair, however, claimed sex with more than 20 couples). Six of the couples only "played" with each other or with couples they had been with on previous occasions. One e-mailer reported that she and her husband "spent most of our time socializing in Las

> *"You just don't see homosexual men at these gatherings." It's considered too creepy, and none of the men in this lifestyle are looking for other men."*
>
> — STEVE

Vegas. We had sex with two new couples and one repeat. We are not the sluts you think we are."

Another respondent, who used to belong to a nudist colony in Pennsylvania, reported that "about 60 percent of the people in the colony were swingers."

"Swinging is no way to fix anything," he wrote, "but it sure can help a good relationship. Although some people want to make swinging this spiritual experience, I like the idea of two people just relaxing into each other. The thing I like as a male is that you can still have the excitement of the 'first time.' That first touch, the first kiss, all the little things that are so much fun and exciting. I have always said that the second time is the best with a partner, because if you are any kind of a caring student you learned about the 'special' places on her body the first time. But it is still new enough to be exciting. And then the great conversations that take place after sex, how we can just relax and talk about almost anything with ease. There's none of the pretense and walls that we build around ourselves every day, just a couple of minutes of freedom."

> *"Swinging is no way to fix anything," he wrote, "but it sure can help a good relationship. Although some people want to make swinging this spiritual experience . . .*
>
> —Anonymous

Yet another wrote, "There were so many beautiful couples there that we just didn't have time to meet most of them. We did drool a lot at many of them, though, and plan to meet them again."

 132

Chapter 5

Steve said the most disappointing aspect of the Aladdin gathering was that hotel security in the area sectioned off for the Lifestyles Convention was more rigid than in the rest of the hotel. "Many of the women who wore see-through dresses to the costume ball were forced to put on pasties to cover their nipples," he said. "But when they left the ball and went to the bar in the front of the hotel, they took off the pasties and no one said a thing. I doubt if we'll be going back to the Aladdin anytime soon."

Two weeks later, I spoke with a longtime Las Vegas resident named Byron, who spent less than an hour in one of the Aladdin rooms during the Lifestyles convention, and his experience was 180 degrees removed from that of Steve and his friends. Byron, a handsome black man in his mid 40s and a lifelong Las Vegan, had received a call from a friend in Southern California in late July informing him that he had been having sex with a beautiful woman named Marsha, who was "about 50 but with the looks and body of a late-30s glamour girl." Byron's friend suggested he give Marsha a call and that he was sure Marsha would be happy to hook up with Byron when she came to Las Vegas for the swingers' gathering.

"The first time I spoke with her on the phone, she told me she just loved strong black men with long thick cocks," Byron says. "I had never spoken with anyone quite that direct before."

Byron said Marsha even encouraged him to masturbate during their conversation, while she shared with him many of her sexual experiences and fantasies. "It was great phone sex," he says. "I couldn't wait until she got to Las Vegas to see her."

The second night of the convention, in early August, Byron went to Marsha's room at the Aladdin, knocked and identified himself, and was let in by another black man, who was naked. What Byron saw in the room was as wild as the set of any XXX-rated movie. Marsha was mounted atop a black man on the bed, had the penis of another black man in her hand and a third in her mouth. "There were about 15 people in the room, nearly all men," Byron says. "All the men were black and well endowed, and the two women were white. The only way to describe it was a consensual interracial gang-bang. No one even stopped for a second when I came in except Marsha, who got off the man she was straddling and came over and offered me a kiss on the lips. I turned my cheek," he says. "The whole scene was a little more than I was prepared for."

> ... *after about 15 minutes of what he called "awkward voyeurism," he quietly left.*

Byron didn't take his clothes off, and after about 15 minutes of what he called "awkward voyeurism," he determined the action was a lot heavier than he was prepared for, so he quietly left. "I've seen a lot of wild stuff in my life," he says. "But that scene at the Aladdin tops everything. If I would rate myself as a nine on a sexually liberated scale, those cats were at about 15. In a way, it was very cool to see people that sexually free, but it was a little freaky too."

A week after Byron recounted this story, he called me and said that Marsha was in Las Vegas again and would be happy to "explain herself."

I met her at a rented party house in east Las Vegas the weekend of the Oscar De la Hoya-Shane Mosley fight. She had been sent a plane ticket to fly in from San Diego to "entertain" several men, not for pay but strictly for fun.

A pretty woman, with soft round features that Byron described as giving off "a zaftig appeal," Marsha didn't fit the image of a woman who would take on an entire room full of men. But then what woman outside the world of video pornography does?

She greeted me warmly, offered me a bottle of water and then recounted over the next hour her 35-year history of pushing the boundaries of every sexual envelope imaginable. To fast-forward through her experiences MTV style: her life story would go something like this:

- Busted by a teacher in Boston for kissing and smoking dope with a classmate at age 12 and transferred by her father to a strict Catholic school.

- Made amateur porn films at 16, stopping by a hotel room in her school uniform and performing sex acts with men and women for cash and because "I thought it was fun." She was paid about $400 per loop. She doesn't believe the films were ever distributed commercially because she has tried for years without luck to find copies.

- Her dad died suddenly when she was 16, and left her mother financially strapped with four children. Marsha was basically unsupervised from that point forward. She got pregnant the next year and put her infant son up for adoption. She has spent all of her adult life trying to locate the boy, who turned 34 this past summer.

- In her early 20s she came to Las Vegas, stayed with a girl-friend in the recently opened original MGM Grand (now Bally's), and earned $10,000 for the week turning tricks. "I never saw the sun all week," she says. "We would entertain one or two men at a time, then walk through the casino and attract more. We never stopped screwing or giving blowjobs the entire week. Finally, hotel security stopped us and suggested it might be time to leave town."

After a decade as a call girl in New York, in 1981 Marsha decided to join the Navy. Many of her friends had died of AIDS. "I looked at the Navy as a way to save my life," she says.

She got married soon after enlisting and adapted a fairly traditional lifestyle, giving birth to a son and daughter, but says she never lost her addiction to sex. "I was faithful to my husband for 14 months," she says, "then I started having affairs."

Around seven years ago, when the Internet started to come into popular usage, her ability to share fantasies and nasty chat with strangers totally reignited her sexual spark. She got into swinging in a big way, and found that through swing clubs she could act out her favorite fantasy, having multiple sexual partners, particularly "well hung black men.

"That's what I love to do," she says. "I can do two gang bangs in one day and not get tired."

She talks about her wild activities, which include bondage and discipline and sadism and masochism, with the calmness of a woman telling you she needs to pick up eggs and butter and a gallon of milk on the way home from work.

Chapter 5

"Sex with multiple partners is euphoria," she says. "It's the high that people seek when they shoot heroin into their arm. It creates the feeling that everything is wonderful and at peace with the world. The endorphins kick in and you enter another world, the closest thing to heaven there is."

When I press Marsha to expound on the pleasure she derives from activities that society regards as totally taboo, she says. "When I have all these men around me, totally excited, it's not the conquest of the individual that ignites me because I lose track of how many men I've had. It's that the scene puts you mentally and physically into another aura of pleasure, like the best drug ever invented. Your mind just goes wild, thinking of what's going to happen next. I'm totally addicted to it."

I ask her if she would engage in the same activity with a group of white men. She pauses for a moment and her voice lowers almost to a whisper.

"There's a theory that a lot of women have feelings of insecurity and low self-esteem and don't think they are good enough for white guys," she says, and I sense that she's explaining herself in that summation. "It's a form of racism if you think about it. It's the idea that I deserve a black man, or several black men, but I don't deserve white men."

She talks about her wild activities . . . with the calmness of a woman telling you she needs to pick up eggs and butter and a gallon of milk on the way home from work.

Marsha's friend Linda, a Las Vegas woman who's been in the swinging lifestyle for 20 years, joins us on the patio. She listens for a while then interjects. "If I may, the reason I go to swing clubs is practical," she says. "It eliminates all the hassle and bullshit that goes with dating or hanging out at singles bars playing the games necessary to link up with men. If I'm lonely and horny and go to a bar, a single man will look at me and wonder how to approach me, or we have to go through the miserable first date and boring conversation and all that stuff that goes with breaking the ice. We're both there for the same reason, but it can take forever before you get busy. But if I go to the Red Rooster as a single woman, it's totally obvious why I'm there. I can be fucking a guy I'm attracted to in 20 minutes without all the nonsense and wasted time."

> *"Wild sex scenes happen often in Las Vegas because it's fantasyland. "*
>
> —MARSHA

Linda says she's taken many or her single and divorced women friends — who are worn out with the mating and dating game — to swing clubs, once they get up enough courage. "And they practically always end up going back there. It's just so much easier and more convenient."

Marsha listens attentively, and laughs and nods her head in agreement. "That's really true," she says. "But there's also something about Las Vegas that gets people to loosen up. Wild sex scenes happen often in Las Vegas because it's fantasyland. People feel that this is the place to act out their sexual dreams because they can feel a sense of anonymity here. It's just like that commercial that we see in San Diego all the time. 'What happens in Las Vegas stays in Las Vegas.'"

Exactly.

Flash backward a couple months. I am in the spacious living room of a 6500-square-foot ranch-style house off South Jones Avenue. It is the home and "office" of David and Virginia Cooper, a mid-30s couple who have moved to Las Vegas in the last year from El Paso, Texas, where they owned and operated gentlemen's clubs. Their two little boys, age five and seven, are playing peacefully in the next room.

David is blonde and wiry and handsome in a Billy Idol rock 'n' roll style. He is wearing tight black leather pants with decorative trim that are clearly intended to make a statement, and his short blonde hair is teased and bleached. Virginia is tall and elegant with platinum blonde hair, and when she seats herself for the interview her slit skirt reveals shapely legs up to here! It reminds me of the Sharon Stone scene in *Basic Instinct*, where she dares her interrogators not to look. Both David and Virginia wear their sexuality openly and without a hint of pretense, which is not surprising considering the reason they have relocated to southern Nevada.

The Coopers have opened a swingers' club in their home, but unlike The Red Rooster, their new business, which is called Plush Party, will accept only good looking, fit couples who are willing to pay $200 to be invited to the gatherings.

The website, Plushparty.com, explains all of the ground rules for admittance, such as:

> Every night is reserved for couples and women only. No single men at any time.

> Applicants for admission must attach a recent full-body photo, (clothed), for consideration to be admitted, with no exceptions.

- First and last names must be included, plus city and state of residence, e-mail and phone numbers, height and weight, and age and gender.
- It is explained that guests to Plush Party are predominantly between the ages of 25 and 45, with exceptions above and below, based on appearance.
- Nothing is sold on the premises, no liquor or food is served, drugs are not tolerated, and the $200 donation is just an admission fee to stay within the letter of the law.

There are also cautions about safe sex and the prerequisite that condoms must be used at the party.

Regarding the dress code, once a couple has "passed inspection" and is allowed entrance, the website discourages khaki shorts for men, 'soccer mom' dress for women, or any kind of business attire. PlushParty encourages sexy, expressive, and erotic clothing.

> *While there are elaborate mansions in Los Angeles that host parties for pretty people, the Coopers' venture is the first of its kind in Las Vegas.*

While there are elaborate mansions in Los Angeles that host parties for pretty people, the Coopers' venture is the first of its kind in Las Vegas.

"We've been to The Red Rooster countless times," David says, "and we really like the Borchers, but what they offer leaves a lot to be desired. We felt that if we provided a totally upscale party place with a classy marketing campaign we could distinguish ourselves from the rest."

While David admits that the first six months of operation have been "about a break-even proposition," he feels that as long as they maintain the highest standards their business will grow and be profitable.

Like nearly every other business in town, he says, Plush Party has felt the pinch of the post-9/11 tourist economy and uncertain political conditions around the world. But he feels the affluent clientele they are seeking will find their way to them when the economy stabilizes.

Before relocating to the west side of town in an open and uncongested neighborhood, the Coopers operated a swing club out of a house in Green Valley. The admission was $75. Their former house had 4000 square feet and was far nicer than the glut of rather sleazy swing clubs that have proliferated closer to the center of town, some of which have been closed due to allegations of prostitution. But although business was steady, and no one in their conservative neighborhood raised an eyebrow over their activities, David felt that the patrons they were seeking would willingly pay a higher admission if the location and clientele were even classier. The problem with $75 customers was that they were often just browsers, willing to pay a small price just to check out an erotic new world. But the Coopers wanted upscale players, not just mid-scale gawkers.

That's when David found the two-story house they now occupy, with the seven bedrooms, ornate bar and dance area, and spacious pool and palm trees in the back. Most of the sculptures and paintings in the house depict nude couples embracing or intertwined. If you walked in off the street, you'd know in a matter of seconds that something funky was going on here. With the fancy new digs, David upped the admission fee to $200 because he felt that anyone paying that price would have every intention of partying all the way.

"If you think about it, where else in Las Vegas can you have a great time in a nice environment and have unlimited sex for $200?" he says.

At the time of our interview, the average Plush Party included between five and 10 couples, but David says he could accommodate 50 or more people as long as the quality is maintained. "I want to get it right before I get it busy," he says. "The very reason for having this house and upping the price was so that we could aim more for quality than quantity, but an electric party with 50 to 100 people could be very cool, too."

> *If you walked in off the street, you'd know in a matter of seconds that something funky was going on here.*

Eighty percent of the Coopers' clientele are tourists, who have been drawn either by word of mouth or through the website. The parties typically start at 10 p.m. and action centers around the bar, where people pour drinks from their own bottles and socialize. David says the ice-breaking ceremonies usually last until about 11:30 or midnight, as stragglers come by following dinner on the Strip, or a show, and that it's usually about 1 a.m. before any sex takes place.

Just as at any party, there are those who are low-keyed and those willing to dance with the proverbial lampshade on their head, or in this case, get it on with everyone that's willing.

"A lot of people at swing parties don't want to admit that they are there for sex," David says. "And then there are those who want action the minute they walk in the door. You can never satisfy them. They want to walk in and see a pile of bodies fucking their brains out. Our idea is to provide an atmosphere that is the full spectrum of social entertainment, with good music, good lighting, stimulating conversation, and a totally pleasant and pleasing atmosphere. We want our parties to be like a great party you would go to as a single person where there was going to be attractive people and you knew it could end up in sex. But with ours, it definitely will end up in sex. It's the excitement of new chemistry and the unknown. And we hope at the end of the night you met some exciting new people, had some great sex and that your partner had great sex, and that you'll want to tell others about it and return yourself."

If there are comparisons to be made between Hank and Anna and the Coopers it is that both couples are adventurous, driven to explore their limits, and nearly voracious in pursuit of sex. When asked what kind of women he likes, Hank told me that he goes through phases. "There were times that I craved Asian women, then I had a period when I loved black women, then tall, then short, then large busted. And I had my J-Lo phase where I just had to have women with big butts."

David Cooper told me, "I've always been able to talk women into sex very easily. And I've always wanted to have sex on a daily basis, sometimes several times a day. I didn't really set out to be a swinger, and I certainly didn't have any role models for this, but I'm the kind of person that goes after what I want. I never hold back from desires. I like to push it to the limit, especially when it comes to sex. I see the point where I want to be and I never have given a fuck about what stood between that point and me. We host parties because we love sex and we thought we could build a nice business based on a concept."

Both Anna Malle and Virginia Cooper say they're bisexual, although it's my hunch that Anna is far more actively so than Virginia, but the women have differing opinions about the sexual activity that takes place between women at swinging parties. While Anna and Hank tell me they think that 90 percent of women who swing are bisexual — which is similar to the numbers that the Lifestyles attendees Steve and his wife Allison would put on it — David and Virginia feel that most of the sex between women could be characterized as "performance art," and that it's "basically a show to get the men excited."

> *. . . most of the sex between women could be characterized as "performance art," and it's "basically a show to get the men excited."*

Even Marsha, the self-admitted sex addict who solicits gang-bangs, describes herself as being "party-bi." She says that in a group situation she puts no limits on what she will do with a woman, but adds, "I would never approach a girl on the street, and I would never date a woman. The activity has to take place in a controlled setting."

"You never see two women pair off by themselves in a private room and have wild lesbian sex," Virginia Cooper says. "There's always a man watching who gets off on the fantasy of the two women, so that he can later join in and feel like a king. Or maybe he just wants to watch them and jerk off to it."

Her husband concurs. "Having been in this lifestyle for several years, I can tell you this whole bisexual female thing is a fallacy," he says. "It's total bullshit. And there's also a double standard that is applied to most men. I promise you that when a guy has had his full evening of sex, the last thing he wants to find is his wife having one-on-one sex with another man. In the last month alone I've had two different husbands stop their wives while they were fucking me because the wife was having too much of a good time. I have a very big cock, and I don't know how else to say it, but men are threatened when they see their women having a great time with me. When a man reacts like that, I tell him that's hypocrisy and that he shouldn't be so selfish."

Both couples agree that in the world of swinging it's important that each couple determine the level they are at and express that honestly with others.

"Some couples are just into oral sex and not intercourse," Virginia says. "And it's important to establish where you're at when you meet other couples so there are no misunderstandings.

"We tell people right up front that I'm bisexual and that Hank is only heterosexual and if we're attracted and the other couple is cool to that then we can party," Anna says. "We had one couple we met through the Internet. Her thing was that she wanted to have sex with me and she wanted to suck Hank's dick but she told me I couldn't suck her husband's dick. She was very controlling over him. We took a pass on being with them because they weren't at our level. So it's very important to establish that in the beginning. It's not always easy to find couples that are on the same page as we are."

> *". . . when a guy has had his full evening of sex, the last thing he wants to find is his wife having one-on-one sex with another man."*
>
> — DAVID COOPER

Loss of Virginity Blues

"Phyllis took off her negligee. Her body was shaped like a fire hydrant and she had shaved off her pubic hair. 'Don't worry about getting me pregnant,' she said. The thought had never crossed my mind."

—JOHN GREGORY DUNNE, *VEGAS: A MEMOIR OF A DARK SEASON*

N early every man can share a story about crossing paths with a prostitute at some point in his life. I'm no different.

My encounter occurred the summer that I turned 18, just after graduating from a strict all-boys Jesuit high school in the Pacific Northwest. At the time I was a certifiable, card-carrying, never-been-close, only-reached-third-base twice virgin. And I was none too happy about it.

All the guys in my close circle of friends also wore the capital V on their graduation gowns, or at least so we thought until my best friend Joe finally fessed up some 10 years later with his admission that he'd been getting lucky on a regular basis since the summer of our junior year. But such was the moral climate in our tight circle of Mass-attending cronies that Joe didn't feel he could share that news with us. We'd had so much sexual angst and fear-of-hell rectitude drilled into us since we'd reached puberty that although we talked about the possibility of sex by the day and the hour, and went to bed thinking about it most every night, none of us was willing to admit that we'd so much as copped a feel for fear the others would think less of us.

I clearly recall that the first time my hand ever inched up a girl's blouse and under her bra, I felt compelled the very next morning to enter a confessional at St. Augustine Catholic Church and explain the deed in detail to our parish priest. Of course although the darkened screen separating the confesser from his absolver is supposed to provide a certain measure of privacy, I was certain in my soul that Fr. Buckley knew who was making this horrid admission — one of his first-string Latin-rapping altar boys — and that he never looked at me the same thereafter.

Chapter 6

Anyway, the pent-up hormones apparently were getting the better of us on a hot August day in 1967 when Paul and Joe and I decided that we were going to make the two-hour-plus drive from Spokane to Wallace, Idaho, and see what we were missing. Wallace is a quaint mining town in the northern panhandle of the state, where back-room poker games, illegal slot machines, and illicit sex for profit had been a way of life since the turn of the last century. Indeed, the burg was often called "Little Las Vegas" and was considered a farm club of the major league city to the south, where it was presumed that mortal sin was the main industry.

Men working in the gloomy dankness of Wallace's mines needed to let off serious steam once they were lifted from the bowels of the silver and copper pits. Their release valves were the working girls who found their way to mining country after making the loop through Carson City, Jackson Hole, Portland, and Seattle. Once there, the girls knew that for a few weeks or a month the demand in Wallace was such that they could entertain as many as 20 clients a day if their backs and psyches could handle it. It was blue-collar prostitution to be sure, just ten dollars for a quickie and fifteen for a half-and-half. It was not uncommon for a patron to visit the Oasis Club, relieve some stress, take a beer break at the Silver Dollar Cafe, then go for what was crudely called "sloppy seconds" an hour later down the street at Sugar's.

After my buddies and I had bought the case of beer needed to fortify our resolve to find out first-hand what sex was all about, we realized we had only 18 dollars left amongst us. Which meant that after setting aside gas money to get home, only one of us would be able to cross the Rubicon into manhood. After flipping coins, it was my luck, or should I say misfortune, to get the nod.

The Loss of Virginity Blues

The experience would have been utterly forgettable were it not for the fact that it was my first time. The matronly woman who answered the doorbell at the top of the stairs of the U&I Club was wearing a white nurse's uniform. My first thought was that she was merely the greeter until she pulled me into a side room, took my (our) ten dollars, then had me hold a pan under myself while she washed me with Phisohex, the smell of which permeated the entire building. While she was doing this, I confessed to her that I was a virgin, and that I was very drunk (as though she couldn't tell). In hindsight, this probably was not the smartest thing I'd ever done, but then all the activities leading up to this moment were not exactly Phi Beta Kappa material either.

> *... after setting aside gas money to get home, only one of us would be able to cross the Rubicon into manhood.*

The woman quickly peeled off her uniform, pulled me on top of her, squirmed slightly and provided fake moans for about 30 seconds, then told me we were finished and to be on my way. I didn't put up much resistance because I had no idea what I was supposed to be getting for my money.

The whole process was sort of like buying a first computer: you pay for it because you have heard you can't live without it, but then you get it home and realize you don't have a clue what to do with it. You suspect you may have gotten a raw deal, but you're not quite sure.

As inebriated as I was, I was darned certain I'd gotten a raw deal and that if what I had endured was this thing called sexual intercourse, then my buddies and I had been spending far too much time talking about it and worrying about it. Were it a movie I'd just watched, I'd review it by saying it was a sad story with no real climax.

On the endlessly long drive back to Spokane, the conversation focused on whether I had indeed officially cashed in my cherry. I prefer to this day to think not. As nearly as I can surmise there had been penetration, but I doubt that a trace of DNA could have linked me to the scene.

And ever since that afternoon the scent of Phisohex cleanser instantly transports me back to that day, that hour, that very minute that someone other than myself washed my penis.

I guess at least I have *that* to be grateful for.

My second encounter with a prostitute, some 15 years after that first visit, was more professional, at least on my part. It was for a magazine article titled "The Double Life of a Las Vegas Housewife," which was eventually turned into a three-part newspaper series that was sold around the world. Later on, a screenplay treatment of the story was made into a television movie, but the fact that I didn't get the writer's credit or any of the remuneration from the film is another story and one far too depressing to share in these pages.

Las Vegas was a much smaller town 20 years ago. The population has more than doubled since then, and every phase of life here, even the world's oldest profession, operated on a much smaller scale.

The subject of that article, a woman we'll call Cynthia, had moved to Las Vegas with two young children from San Jose after her marriage to a cop went sour. When she arrived, she had little cash and a lot of debt, but she was a registered nurse and knew she could scrape out a living. However, the medical profession was plan B. Plan A was to see if she could make her living as a call girl. She didn't know anybody here, and had no idea where to start or even if she could handle the emotional weight of crossing the line into prostitution. And she'd never made love even once with a man she wasn't somewhat attracted to.

I remember being incredulous, when I met her, that anyone could make that leap on a whim. But she figured she could, because she loved sex and felt it was the only way she could make enough money to provide well for her children and be closely involved with the daily events of their lives.

> ## "I realized if I shut my eyes a body was a body. But I also determined that I was never going to do it for free again."
>
> – CYNTHIA

"My first time was a freebie with a bellman at the Las Vegas Hilton," she told me. "He said he could refer me to a lot of hotel guests if I was worth the money. He was kinda ugly, short and bald, but I did it. And I found there was nothing to it," she said. "I realized if I shut my eyes a body was a body. But I also determined that I was never going to do it for free again."

Cynthia was pragmatic about her job and its role in Las Vegas society. "In this town, the economy is based on gambling and women," she said. "We are an economic necessity. If you busted all the working girls and top-dollar call girls you'd have a ghost town here with mobile-home drivers just stopping for gas and to play the nickel slots."

She also claimed that law enforcement in the early 1980s was not in the least concerned about women like her. "The political officials and police are concerned with street hookers who are rolling the johns," she said. "I think it's disgusting. Look at the girls on the corner of Flamingo and the Strip, hanging out and harassing married men with their wives right beside them. Now that's a problem for the city's image."

The following year, when long-time Metro officer John Moran ran for Sheriff with the promise that he was going to clean the hookers off the street, he won resoundingly and Cynthia voted for him.

"I may be a prostitute," she told me, "but I don't consider myself anywhere near those ladies. Those crack whores are trying to victimize men. I satisfy them."

And so Cynthia had a three-year run as a hooker in Las Vegas. During that time, she also worked part-time as a nurse, and she even ministered to several victims of the devastating MGM Grand fire in 1980. She also led her daughter's Brownie Girl Scout troop and coached her son's peewee baseball team. Meanwhile, it took her only six months to develop her own clientele of customers who would come to town three or four times a year, and pay her $350 per session or $1,000 for all night. Cynthia would not do out-of-town gigs, because she didn't want to leave her kids for more than a day at a time. In 1981, the year before our interview, Cynthia had earned $38,000 and worked fewer than 50 days. She stayed in the business another three years, then went back to medical school and became a doctor. She now practices in the Eastern U.S. and sends me a Christmas card every year.

Cynthia may have been the most honest interview subject I ever met. As she revealed her stories to me, I felt like I was being allowed to look at an x-ray of her soul. I was to learn in my conversations with other women of the world's oldest profession, that they also were dying to tell their stories, and they too would hold nothing back.

The Mother Hen

"*I had never subscribed to the youthful bravado that paying for it was slightly less satisfying than jerking off. I did like talking to hookers, I think out of some residual Catholic impression that as long as one did not handle the merchandise, one was committing only a venial and not a mortal sin.*"

— John Gregory Dunne, Vegas: *A Memoir of a Dark Season*

There was something raging inside Karin from the time she reached puberty. All young girls and boys are curious about sex and the human body as they grow into early adulthood, but she was nearly obsessed by it.

She would borrow her brother's Playboy magazines and stare by the hour at pictures of naked women. She admired the photography, marveled at the beauty of the women, at times even lusted for them. This caused her to wonder about the true nature and direction of her sexual urges. She liked boys as well, but her desires were conflicted and fluctuating. She didn't feel she could talk to her friends about sex, and certainly not her devoutly Catholic mother, who with her husband had adopted Karin as a six-year-old and rescued her from the revolving door life of orphanages and foster families. But her father had died just six years after the adoption, when she was 12, and the girl's adolescent years created tensions with her mother, who had more than she could handle carrying on alone.

As Karin grew older and played volleyball in college, she discovered that her coach and most of her teammates were gay, and some of them pursued her aggressively. She found this a big turnoff. On one hand she liked that the girls found her attractive, but the paradox was that she didn't want things to go further.

She knew that men were going to be a big part of her life, and that sexual behavior was going to play a major role, but the tug of desire was offset by the warnings of her Catholic schoolteachers. In college Karin wore her thick black hair pulled back and hardly ever wore makeup, yet she was constantly being pursued, by both men and women. Suitors were drawn by her olive complexion, pretty smile, and big brooding eyes. And she had an unfiltered laugh that could fill a room with its exuberance.

As she approached the age of 20, Karin learned to be more open in discussing sex with her college friends, but she would not totally understand the origin of her obsession with it for another 15 years, when she was compelled to trace her birth roots back to a small village in Germany. But we'll get to that later.

Karin read everything she could about sex. Sheri Hite's bestseller, *What Women Want,* was a particular favorite. She also loved romance novels, and far more prurient literature that described every detail of sexual intimacy.

"I wondered why my friends talked about sex only occasionally, when for me it was a constant preoccupation," she says, speaking with me in the summer of 2003. We are seated in a lovely anteroom at her beautiful Mediterranean-style home in a gated community on Las Vegas' east side. The home is richly decorated in earth tones, with luxurious furnishings, and is cleaned to a shine. It's evident that Karin has come a long way from her early years in California. She is today a single mother of two, and is proud of the tiled roof she has put over their heads and the financial freedom that allows her to spend all those 'quality-time' occasions with them.

She knows too well what it's like to struggle financially, and she feels she's more than paid her dues to achieve her current status. Karin, you see, is probably the most successful madam in Las Vegas,

> *"I wondered why my friends talked about sex only occasionally, when for me it was a constant preoccupation,"*
>
> — KARIN

although she hates the term commonly used to describe her profession. She prefers to say that she owns and operates a high-class adult entertainment business. She has been kidded about being the "Heidi Fleiss of Las Vegas" because she entertains some of the city's richest and most celebrated visitors.

She giggles at the comparison, and says she wishes she made the kind of money that Heidi made in her heyday, but boasts that the 15 women who work for her regularly are just as pretty as Heidi's girls and every bit as effective at fulfilling their clients' fantasies.

Lack of money became a big issue for Karin when she was 20 years old. She was taking classes at two different universities in Southern California and still living at home with her mom. She recalls it as an extremely stressful time.

"I started dating an extremely well-educated and interesting black man that I'd met at the university, and my mother freaked out and couldn't handle it," she says. "To her, interracial dating was totally taboo. I rebelled and told her that if she would not accept me for who I was then I was going to leave. And when no one else in my family came to my defense, that was very disturbing. So for a time, I was disenfranchised from this good woman who had adopted me."

Karin broke from any semblance of a traditional life style at that point, and decided to rely on her survival instincts, wherever fate led. Shortly, she realized that she needed more income to continue her education. In scanning the classified ads in the *Los Angeles Times* one day she saw an ad that said, "Girls, Girls, Girls! $750 per week!"

The ad led her downtown Los Angeles and the Starlight Club.

"If you've ever listened to the song, 'Private Dancer,' Tina Turner describes the situation perfectly," she says. "It was an Asian social club, run by a totally Oriental staff with a mama-san. They had about five beautiful Asian girls and the rest of us were Americans, most of us college students. It was all about socializing with these Asian clients, and dancing with them. There was no alcohol, no touchy-feely or nudity or anything like that. You just put your time card in a clock and when some man chose you from behind the glass you danced with him. The men came in there to get away with touching a woman's body without it being illegal. On a good week, I could make up to $750, but after awhile I was repulsed by these men holding me so close. It certainly wasn't glamorous, and there was a real lonely side to it all, but that marked my entry into the world of adult entertainment."

As Karin recounts her story, her feet are curled up beneath her and there's a note of melancholy in her voice. She tells me she's intrigued with recreating this story for a stranger, that it's causing her to think about those early days that have been shoved into a dark attic of her mind. But it's clear that she considers all her decisions along the way as building blocks of the confidence required to start her own business and attain her present comforts.

Her first act of sexual intercourse for direct pay occurred during her time at the social club.

"He was an older gentleman, about 50, and the nicest guy in the world," she says. "He would come in every night just to see me. He brought me gifts, and he'd take me to dinner and at times he would pay me not to go in to work, which was an option I far preferred because even the smell of the men's cologne was starting to repulse me. One night I was in this gentleman's Jacuzzi with him drinking champagne, and I started to feel like I was falling for him. He was a classy guy and was in a way becoming a father figure to me."

Karin had it in mind to make love with him that evening, when suddenly he said he would take care of her financially to be with him sexually. When he offered to pay $500 to have sex with her that very night, she remembers being very excited to be getting a lot of money for doing something she was about to do for free.

"That was the night that entirely changed my life," she says. "How did I feel? I felt great. I felt powerful. And really for the first time in my life I felt totally in control of my situation. He actually cooked breakfast for me the next morning."

> ## "How did I feel? I felt great. I felt powerful. I felt totally in control of my situation.
>
> –KARIN

Karin saw him professionally for an entire year, several times a week, and he paid her $500 every single time.

She says the single biggest misperception from women who have never sold sex for money is that doing so cheapens a woman or makes her feel compromised. "It's quite the opposite," she says. "I feel empowered every time. I feel attractive and desirable and valuable. I never feel cheap. I feel expensive."

She used the money from her first professional client to pay her tuition and other bills. "I knew too well what it was to be starving to death and to live in a little one-bedroom apartment with a girl-friend in a twin bed," she says. "When I started making good money I looked at it as my easy way out from the real world and fighting poverty. And that was a liberating feeling."

The relationship with the man soon became complicated. "When you're younger you kind of fall in love with your clients," Karin says. "You have so much appreciation for what the man's doing for you, and in his case I respected him as well, but as time goes on it starts to turn. I see it now as an occupational hazard of my business. After a while the man becomes cheaper and resentful of having to pay you each time, and when that happens you lose respect for him. And the sex goes from something that has some caring behind it, to telling yourself, 'I need to fuck this guy because I want the money.' And it eventually gets tiresome and boring for both of you. But we parted friends. He was good for me at the time and he made me realize I could do this as my profession and be totally okay with it.

"I know people are shocked when they hear this, but I just don't have an ounce of guilt about what I do. It's adult entertainment, the oldest profession in the world, and it's never going away. And when I realized I could be really good at it I felt totally free from my financial worries."

Karin eschews the word "prostitute" entirely in describing her profession. "That word is not in my vocabulary," she says. "That's a word that people use to demean our profession. I use the term "working girl" because what I do is contract for work and I'm getting paid for it."

> *"I feel empowered every time. I feel attractive and desirable and valuable. I never feel cheap. I feel expensive."*
>
> –KARIN

About the time her first sex-for-hire arrangement was ending, Karin was talking to one of her co-workers at the social club, and the girl encouraged her to become a stripper, saying that she could earn $300 to $400 a night dancing, easily doubling her income. Karin didn't think she could do it; she felt that the strip-club scene was seedy. But when she went to the club, a place called the Jet Strip located near the LAX Airport, she was shocked by what she saw.

"This absolutely gorgeous woman with an amazing body was on stage dancing, and there was money all over the stage," she recalls. "I could not believe that anyone this beautiful was taking off her clothes for a living. The club was also tastefully decorated. Compared to where I was working, it was heaven."

The owner of the club, which served only juice and soft drinks and therefore could legally allow girls to dance totally nude, approached Karin, told her she was beautiful, and asked if she could start working that very night. She told him she didn't think she could do it. Undaunted, he offered her a job as a bartender, and said if she changed her mind she could become a dancer later on.

"I took the job because I wanted to be in that environment," she says. "I was just drawn to a business that was adult-oriented and based on sex. It was in my blood somehow, I wasn't certain why."

When I inquired whether any of her customers from the Asian social club followed her to the Jet Strip, she had a surprising answer. "Even though I asked several of them to come visit me there, not a single one of them did," she says. "It was a totally different mentality that brought those men to the social club. They wanted that one-on-one slow dancing and the physical contact. They felt I was exploiting myself working at the nude club."

Karin started to develop her own personal clientele as a bartender. Just as a woman in a bikini will draw the most attention at a nudist colony, so the men were intrigued by the one woman in the place who kept her clothes on. She provided a sense of mystery lacking in the other women. Finally, one customer couldn't stand it any longer. He offered her a thousand dollars on the spot if she would take off her clothes and dance. She told him the only way she could do it was if he went to a liquor store and bought her some vodka. She knew she couldn't do it sober, so after a few quick cocktails she went onstage and did her thing. The men went nuts.

"That was it for me," she says with a big smile. "When I saw how much attention that got me, I was hooked. I felt wonderful up there, like a movie star, and I discovered that night that I was an exhibitionist."

Just then, she's interrupted by a call on her cell phone. It's one of her girls, having boyfriend problems. She patiently spends about 10 minutes on the call, consoling the girl, telling her that she's inevitably going to have to break off the relationship, that the guy is basically pimping off her earnings.

He offered her a thousand dollars on the spot if she would take off her clothes and dance.

After she hangs up, she shakes her head. "About half the time the boyfriends of these girls just become bums," she says. "But it's hard to live totally alone in this business. I see the need to have someone to go home to after a tough gig, but it's hard to find a really good man who can understand what we do and still maintain his own identity."

Quickly, we're back to her story:

Karin's girlfriend who had coaxed her into visiting the strip club was correct about the income at the Jet Strip. She started making $300 a day and more when she danced, and this from working the less lucrative day shift. It was the most money she'd ever earned, and she celebrated by cutting back to working four days a week. She also quit school. She knew in her heart even then that her future was going to be in adult entertainment, and the strain of going to college and working full time just didn't seem worth it anymore. For the first year or so, she didn't do tricks with customers, either. She says she went through a series of boyfriends, all men she had met at the club.

"Once I started dancing, my entire life revolved around everybody I met in the club," she says. "Those were the people I dated, the people I socialized with. The club employees and regulars became my family, and the only thing that ever troubled me was the fact that my life choices never gave me any sense of guilt. That sounds funny, I know. But I just felt perfectly comfortable and natural in the world of sex and adult entertainment. I had known since I was a teenager that this was the career path I would follow."

> ## "I had known since I was a teenager that this was the career path I would follow."
>
> – KARIN

After a couple of years at the club, Karin bought her first townhouse. She was always looking at ways to invest wisely. She had essentially been on her own since she was 18, and didn't want to ever again scrounge for money. She spent her off hours reading, mainly romance novels and self-help books. She studied metaphysics, read books on health and nutrition, and attended seminars and occasional retreats. She worked hard at keeping her head in a good place and not falling into the depression and drug and alcohol problems that were fairly common with other dancers. She felt validated by the money she was making, and knowing she was good at her job. Occasionally, she got gigs that took her overseas, and says some of her most loyal customers would even follow her to Japan and Europe to watch her dance. Gradually, she resumed sex-for-hire. She would occasionally have sex with a drop-in customer at the club who made her a good offer, but she drew the line at regulars, those men who made up what might be called her fan base.

"If you sleep with a good customer who's been coming in night after night and tipping you well, you'll lose that customer," she says. "The whole art of stripping is fantasy, the art of building and maintaining desire in a man. But once he's had you, he'll stop coming in to see you. The fantasy is gone and the income stops. So I was very picky about the customers I slept with."

She enjoyed the tease game that runs through the strip club scene. If a customer begged her for sex, she would pretend she would never consider it, that she was a good girl, and that of course made her that much more desirable to the customer, who would then place a higher value on that which he couldn't have. Karin understood that the more untouchable she appeared to the men, the more they would tip her and the more they would be willing to pay eventually to fulfill their fantasy.

> "*The whole art of stripping is fantasy, the art of building and maintaining desire in a man.*"
>
> – KARIN

Karin estimates that she was earning from $150,000 to $200,000 through those early years. She picked her jobs carefully, and there was little she wouldn't try if she felt the money was good and the circumstances relatively safe. For a time she danced once a week at a lesbian club in Hollywood called Peanuts. She was paid $500 a shift plus tips. Then another dancer introduced her to the dominatrix scene.

"She taught me how really successful men often have a need to be dominated," she says. "This was another amazing facet of adult entertainment to me because there is no sexuality involved. It is strictly imagination and creativity and acting. The woman and I would do shows in San Francisco for good money. I played the submissive and she played the dominatrix. We did it for a year, but I found I didn't enjoy it because I don't like being vulnerable. I like being in control, and I had to sacrifice that while I was involved in that scene."

As Karin reached her late 20s, she felt at peace with her life; she enjoyed her work and continued to sock away money. Increasingly, when she would have sex with a client, questions would come up about other girls. Could she bring another girl, maybe a tall blonde, the next time? Could she put together several girls for a bachelor party? She knew other girls who were "moonlighting" on the side, and it seemed that more and more often she was pulling other girls from the club to do small parties or simply a two-on-one arrangement. She was a good organizer, and she was growing tired of giving away this marketable skill. She had been acting in the role of a madam, without receiving a commission.

Around 1990, after eight years in adult entertainment, she decided to form a business. She would find women she could count on for appointments, and she would take a percentage, initially just 20 percent of what she booked. All of her business was generated in the Redondo, Newport Beach, and Hermosa Beach area near Orange County.

Her fee for each girl attending a bachelor party was $300. The job mainly called for stripping and lap dancing, but any services the girl elected to perform beyond that were her choice, and the additional

Chapter 7

money was hers to keep. She called her business Bachelor Fantasy and ran it for a year.

By not hiring security to escort the girls to and from these parties, Karin admits, she was taking risks. She says she has always relied on her gut instincts in judging men, and it was her method to ask a lot of questions on the phone when a party was being arranged. Only once did she feel her life was in danger. At a bachelor party with more than two dozen men, one was crazed on drugs and got very aggressive, holding her against her will. She broke free long enough to call a boyfriend.

"I said, 'You better get over here right now. I don't think I'm going to get out of here.' And I told him to make sure he had his gun because he might have to kill somebody.

"My friend arrived quickly and he played it out really cool. He calmly came into the room and said, 'Hey guys, I hope everyone is having a good time. I'm just here to see that the girls are okay.' And then he came into a back room where the wacko had me and he threw him down and put him in a scissor lock and almost killed him. The guy was turning red and was totally out of breath. There was no other way to stop him. He was like an enraged bull."

Karin says the only time men at these parties get unruly is when the girls get ready to leave. She says they never get too rough during sex, but they are sometimes disappointed when their time is up and the party's over. She admits she's been fortunate never to have been hurt.

"In all honesty, I can't believe I'm alive to tell you these stories," she says. "I probably should be dead. I have been in situations where there were guys smoking crack or using methamphetamines and they can get pretty stupid, but I've always been good at talking myself into and out of situations. I guess it's just another occupational hazard of the profession, but human behavior can get fairly unpredictable when sex and passion are involved. And there's a lot of passion in my business."

Then one night on a dance engagement in Las Vegas, at the Palomino Club in North Las Vegas, Karin met a man who would redirect her life. He was also in the adult business, and although she said it was an unlikely match, she fell in love with him. She moved to Las Vegas in the late 1980s, they were married, and within a couple years had two children.

> *". . . human behavior can get fairly unpredictable when sex and passion are involved. And there's a lot of passion in my business."*
>
> —KARIN

When she left Southern California, Karin sold her new business for $20,000 cash. She took a hiatus from the adult business during her marriage and child-bearing years, and thought she was re-tired to the responsibilities of housewife. But after five years, when the marriage ended in divorce, she sensed that her best method of providing for the children was to return to the business she knew best. And when she came out of retirement, it was with a clear head and a resolve to build a strong business in a city that understood perhaps better than anyplace else what adult entertainment and fantasy is all about.

In her years here, Karin had learned that Las Vegas was not only a better market than Southern Cal for managing working girls, but

Chapter 7

possibly the best market in the country. Sure, Heidi Fleiss and, before her, a woman named Madame Alex, had made a fortune catering to the desires of the rich and famous in Hollywood. But Karin didn't want to run a huge business, nor one that would inspire so much curiosity from the authorities. Clearly, it was overexposure that had gotten Heidi in trouble. When too many people are sharing too much information about a business that is against the law, it draws the attention of law enforcement agents, who don't appreciate being publicly embarrassed.

But Karin knew that sex was on the minds of millions of business travelers, conventioneers, golfers, and gamblers who come to Las Vegas each year, and if she ran a first-class service with the hottest women imaginable, she could make a great living.

Las Vegas was not only a better market than Southern Cal, but possibly the best market in the country.

After a short stint dancing at Glitter Gulch, a gentlemen's club located under the Fremont Street Experience canopy, Karin had found about 25 girls who wanted to work part-time or full-time for her. Her prices starting out were $300 to $500 per girl per hour, but in the beginning she kept only 20 percent of their earnings. This would change after her first year in business.

The typical bachelor party works something like this: two girls are hired to work the party, which takes place in a nice suite or penthouse at a Strip hotel. Most of the details have been discussed earlier by the man arranging the party and Karin. Often the man will request a blonde and a brunette, or two blondes. "My clients do not like the slutty, come-fuck-me look," she says. "They want the girl next door or the *Playboy* centerfold look. And the vast majority, about ninety percent, request blondes."

Karin has explained to the client prior to arrival exactly what the girls will and will not do. The rules are simple: no kinky sex, no bathroom stuff, no anal sex, no violence of any kind, condoms are mandatory, cash must be paid up front, no credit cards or checks accepted, and so on. Once the deal has been arranged, she'll call the room on her cell phone, just minutes before the girls arrive, to make sure everyone is ready. This is a business conducted on the clock, so punctuality is paramount.

> *"Men are absolutely stupefied when they see pussy. Their brains go flying out the window."*
>
> –KARIN

The girls start by introducing themselves to the clients and exchanging idle chitchat about where the men are from and how they're doing gambling. Then they'll perform a girl-girl show, dancing to music that they have brought, then engage in sex play with each other, kissing, oral sex (if the girls are comfortable with each other), then playing with sex toys.

"It's amazing to watch men's eyes when they see this," Karin says. "Men are absolutely stupefied when they see pussy. Their brains go flying out the window."

The bachelor is then blindfolded, and the girls flirt with him and give him a lot of personal attention in front of his friends. If the bachelor wants something more, this is negotiated, usually beforehand, and then he'll depart with one or both of the girls into a room adjoining the suite and get down to business.

Chapter 7

"Nine times out of ten, the bachelor does not want full-service sex," says Karin. "Either he's had too much to drink, or he can't handle the peer pressure, or he simply doesn't want to cheat on his bride-to-be. There are times the bachelor is dying to fuck the girls, but he's afraid the incident will come back to haunt him."

Unless there is a preponderance of drugs or alcohol, the men are usually so worked up after the girl/girl show that it doesn't require much time to satisfy them. Many times, says Karin, a man will reach orgasm during oral sex. In more cases than not, actual intercourse never takes place. It never turns into an outright orgy, with several couples having sex in the same room. The suites or penthouses usually contain enough rooms so that everyone can do their thing with a measure of privacy.

Just like every other commodity, sex for hire has experienced inflation in the last decade. Karin would have sex with men in the 1980s for $300. In the '90s the price went up to $500, and since 2000 she and her girls get $1,000 an hour. She says that she lost very few customers when she raised her prices. She merely upgraded her clientele to more affluent, generally classier men.

"Some of the men at five hundred dollars expected you to do a back flip for the money," she says, laughing. "Or they wanted anal sex, which we don't do. Once I got smart and jacked up my prices, I discovered that the men who would pay $1,000 were much nicer. I try to add little touches that separate my business from others. For instance, I have some good wines, I collect them, and every time I'm with a new client I'll give him a good bottle of wine to take home to remember me by.

"I had a client last night who was with a friend. They wanted four girls for three hours. You do the math. We were paid twelve thousand dollars, of which I kept six."

Just then, her cell phone rings for a second time. "I'm sorry," she says. "I have to take this one, too. It's a logistics situation." She then coaches one of her girls who is having problems making a flight connection to an important weekend gig. Karin gives her some practical advice about checking the airline for other connections, then she signs off with, "And don't worry about it. You're going to have a great time. These are good guys."

She takes just one other call this night, from her niece who handles phone reservations for her. "She wants to get into the business full-time," she says. "It's very intoxicating once a girl sees the money that can be made."

> ## "It's very intoxicating once a girl sees the money that can be made."
>
> —KARIN

A lot of Karin's conversation with me is understandably off the record. She rattles off the names of good customers who are A-list movie stars or professional athletes. I am surprised at the names of many, who have managed to mold reputations as happily married, clean-cut citizens.

"You shouldn't be surprised," she says. "Imagine if you made millions of dollars making movies or playing sports, and could spend just a tiny fraction of that money to have safe sex with a beautiful woman with a terrific body. It doesn't mean you don't love your wife. It's simply another form of entertainment."

She then mentions a formerly married Hollywood couple, superstars both, who used to share her girls. "The wife was a real freak," she says. "She liked girls every bit as much as her husband."

I comment that the supermarket tabloids would probably pay her a king's ransom for verifiable proof of her claims.

"I'm not ready to retire yet," she says, laughing. Then in a serious tone, adds, "Of course I'd never publicly divulge the name of a client. That would be an act of betrayal, and very bad for business."

⚓

While the months around the turn of the millennium were extremely profitable for Karin, her business, like so many others in Las Vegas, was hit hard after the tragedy of 9/11. She says her income was cut in half the following year. "I had 30 girls working fairly regularly for me before then," she says. "I now have 15. Some of my clients died in the World Trade Center. They were wonderful people. Then the stock market dove, and with those two things happening at the same time I would really have been hurt had I not been frugal and saved a lot of money."

The rules of supply and demand, and a plodding economy, caused Karin to offer specials. "I offered my thousand-dollar clients two girls for $1,500, giving them a little price break," she says. "Whenever I do this, though, I take the hit myself. I don't cut it out of the girl's income. But I can feel my business coming back strong now."

Karin says the key to her developing such a strong business in a short time was her ability to meet a lot of casino reps, casino hosts, and hotel VIPs up to the top level. "Every weekend for several months starting out I would get all dolled up and go to the hotels and meet these people," she says. "And I would introduce myself to them and give them my business card and explain that I was operating an adult entertainment business and that I would like to do business with them. Some wouldn't take my card, and others would say, 'Okay, great.' It wasn't much different than the first year of starting any business. It was a lot of hard work, and getting out there among the right people, but the edge I had was that I knew I had a great product and that the demand for it would never go out of fashion.

> "I knew I had a great product and that the demand for it would never go out of fashion."
>
> –Karin

"Once I went to a *Playboy* Magazine party at a large hotel, and one of the hosts called me and invited me to bring some of my girls to the party," she says. "We all went, and when I walked in with this entourage of gorgeous women you could see the jaws drop. I really worked the room that night and told all these VIPs that my girls were available for full-service adult entertainment. And the response was disbelief that women this beautiful were available for a fee. I generated a lot of business and contacts just from that one evening."

There are two ways that Karin finds her girls. More than half find her, by hearing about her through the grapevine, or from a girlfriend who works for her and is making good money. She also occasionally talks to sales clerks in the stores she frequents. More than once, a pretty clerk has inquired of Karin about her occupation, and she'll be direct with them. She says these girls are never shocked by her answer, because "Hey, this is Las Vegas. No one is that naïve."

If the girl isn't instantly turned off by the idea, Karin says she will say something like, "If you ever want to make some serious money, rather than just scraping by, give me a call."

Usually, the girl will say something like, "Oh, I could never do that," or "That's interesting, but I don't think it's for me." And most times, it isn't. But maybe the girl wouldn't object to being paid for going out for the evening just to be eye candy at a corporate party. If she chooses to do that, which is really not much different than a modeling job at a convention, she can make about two or three hundred for the evening, far more than she's earning in her eight-hour shift at the store.

"Some of the girls are willing to go to a function and hang out with wealthy clients and let guys flirt with them," says Karin. "But then they'll talk to some of my other girls and find out about the real money that's out there. A lot of times I can ease them into the business that way. I approach it real indirectly."

Recently, two UNLV students, both 18, were referred to Karin. They were intrigued with the fantasy of being call girls, of a quick and exciting way of paying their tuition and socking away some money. Karin said one of them was really cute, and the other had a beautiful face but was overweight. "She was an Anna Nicole Smith type," she says, "before she got really heavy. These girls wanted to do a little package deal, always working together, and I told the heavy girl that although she was young and beautiful — two things that men crave — she had to lose some weight. I was totally frank and said that at her current weight I couldn't send her to one of my jobs. The two ended up getting in an argument with each other over it, so I don't know what will happen. But for me to maintain the standards of my business, my girls have to be beautiful, tremendously sexy, and have class. And they can't be chubby. They need to be built like a brick shithouse."

There is always some training required for a new girl. If a girl is beautiful with a great body but not as experienced sexually as Karin would prefer, she'll provide some instruction. Whether it's demonstrating oral sex techniques on a banana, or just talking for hours with the girl about how to handle different situations, she has to quickly bring a new girl up to the expectations of a client willing to spend big money on her. "One of the first questions my girls will ask a client they haven't been with before is 'What do you like?' Karin says. "And if he's too shy to tell her, then she'll start performing oral sex on him, and ask him to tell her if she's doing a good job.

> ## *"They need to be built like a brick shithouse."*
>
> —Karin

"I'll send a new girl out with one that has a lot of experience, so she can watch and follow that girl's lead," she says. "Then I'll get a full report the next day on how everything went. I typically get ninety percent raves, men calling and thanking me for how terrific and sexy my girls were. The complaints I get are usually the guy's fault. Sometimes he's had too much cocaine, or too much Ecstasy, or too much alcohol, and he can't perform, so he blames the girl. But that's only a small percentage of the time."

Karin insists that her operation be the absolute best in Las Vegas, and that means having the sexiest women behaving with style and poise. "I want my girls to be totally classy until they get in the bedroom," she says. "Then they can be as nasty as they want to be. The client usually likes to hear dirty talk, and have the girl do things he doesn't get at home from his wife. Obviously, if he was getting everything he needed on the home front, he wouldn't have any use for our services."

The single most important physical requirement for one of Karin's girls is that she have a terrific body. "If a good looking girl comes to me and has natural breasts that don't look good or her teeth are crooked, I'll tell her to go get some boobs or get her teeth straightened and then we'll talk. But if she's still interested I might start her on the lower end jobs and keep half her money towards her future dental or cosmetic surgery bills. I've made that agreement with girls several times, as a way of forcing them to hold onto the money they'll need for the improvements."

> "I want my girls to be totally classy until they get in the bedroom."
>
> –KARIN

While in 2003 Karin was still feeling the pinch of 9/11, nationwide travel cutbacks, the war in Afghanistan and Iraq, and other elements beyond her control, she feels the next two years should bring terrific business.

"The economy in Las Vegas has picked up," she says. "There are a couple of great new hotels on the horizon, and overall I've never had a better-looking, sexier group of girls than I have now. So I'm really optimistic."

There is something else that has perked up Karin's spirits. And it occurred last summer, totally out of the blue, and answered nagging questions about who she was and why her life led her down these unlit roads. They were questions she thought would never be answered until she went on an Internet search and hired professionals to help her discover the identity of her birth mother, who had given her up for adoption 40 years before.

Within three months, they had located her mother in a small village outside Hamburg, Germany. The woman, then 55 years old, got hysterical when she was contacted and told about the woman in Las Vegas who was searching for her. Verification was made through a series of questions. For instance, the woman was able to report that her infant daughter had suffered a burn mark on one leg while in a German orphanage. Shortly after, Karin flew to Germany and had an emotional reunion with her mother.

"We look alike," Karin says. "She was so emotional and happy to see me. But she also told me she hates herself for not keeping me. It has plagued her for her entire life."

The story of Karin's unfortunate early years unraveled over the next several days and weeks, and into the summer. Karin even flew her mother to Las Vegas last summer for two months so they could really get to know each other. She learned that the woman had gotten pregnant when she was just 16, by a 25-year-old man who had a good job in a factory. The girl was hoping the pregnancy would convince the man to marry her, but he declined. Living in humble circumstances with her mother and aunt, who were angry about her pregnancy and threw her out of the house, the girl considered suicide, even buying pills at a store to end her life. But she didn't have the nerve to follow through. Eventually, a policeman found her walking the streets of Hamburg, despondent, and returned her home. The mother and aunt begrudgingly took her back in, but as church-going Catholics, they wouldn't concede to an abortion. So the girl had the baby, a daughter, who was placed in an orphanage. From there, the baby girl was moved around to a number of foster homes, and eventually when she was five she was brought to the U.S., where an ad with her picture was placed in the *Los Angeles Times*. Karin was adopted from that ad.

"I've read a lot about reunions like mine with my mother," Karin says, her voice growing quieter. "And they're difficult. Part of me is extremely angry at her for not toughing it out and keeping me. Our relationship got difficult after she was with me for a few weeks last summer. But I did learn something that gave me some peace about my inclination from a young age to make my living in adult entertainment. I learned that my real mother became a prostitute after she gave me up for adoption, and that her own mother — my grandmother — had been a prostitute as well. I found out that this business is in my blood, going back three generations. I didn't find any of this out until I'd been in the business for nearly 20 years.

"This discovery has helped me learn who I really am, after all."

I'll Be Watching You

"This is one of the hallmarks of Vegas hospitality. The only bedrock rule is Don't Burn the Locals. Beyond that, nobody cares. They would rather not know. If Charlie Manson checked into the Sahara tomorrow morning, nobody would hassle him as long as he tipped big."

— Hunter S. Thompson, *Fear and Loathing in Las Vegas*

The year is 1993. An undercover vice crew from the Las Vegas Metropolitan Police Department, led by Lieutenant Bill Young, is setting up a hooker sting in a Strip hotel. They hope to bust an outcall dance service, one of those hydra-headed fronts for prostitution that will occupy 100 pages of advertising in the July Sprint phone book 10 years later. Young has been getting far too many complaints across his desk in recent weeks, and it's time to stir the pot. The sting operation is being filmed for a television series called *American Detective*. The show's host is John Bonnell, a silver-haired, square-jawed former sheriff from Oregon who narrates those police-chase videos that air at all hours on cable stations.

The sting is arranged among Young and four other Metro cops, including Korean detective Jason Hahn in the role of a big-spending businessman looking for action. Central casting couldn't have chosen a better leading man for this reality show than Bill Young. He has the looks and demeanor to host his own television series, should that be on his agenda, but he has more ambitious plans.

Young's smooth voice is heard over aerial shots of the Strip. "People come out to Las Vegas and they think Wow, this is a wild and fast and loose town, and in some ways it is. But most girls who come here and get involved in prostitution don't have anything. Most of them have drug problems, and most of them have pimps."

Young's voiceover explains that the prostitute doesn't fear going to jail nearly as much as what her pimp will do to her if she cops a plea and rolls over on him. And yet that's just what Metro wants these girls to do once they're busted. The idea is to move up the chain and nail the bigger fish running these operations, which generate millions of dollars a year for the bigger companies.

As Young and his crew watch a TV monitor from an adjoining room, the hidden camera records Hahn negotiating sex with an on-call girl named Stacey, an attractive, busty brunette with the sweet face of a 4-H queen. He plays his part perfectly, even pretending to need a Korean-English dictionary to communicate with her. This cracks up Young, who says, "We're even playing Pictionary tonight."

Stacey tells Hahn that she'll do whatever he wants for $500. She even agrees to let him videotape her as she takes off her clothes. From the adjoining room, Young says, "The pictures provide better evidence for the judge." As Stacey removes her panties and stands naked waiting for the fun to begin, Jason says in his contrived accent, "I love America, I love America."

This is the tip-off phrase that he has enough evidence for an arrest, and Bill Young and his fellow cops hustle into the room. "We love America, too," Bill says. "And you are busted."

Stacey immediately breaks into tears and is shaking. Young has her put her clothes on and then tries to calm her down. His manner is totally professional, but he shows compassion. She's not the hardened hooker he so often runs into. Stacey tells him she doesn't have a pimp and that this is her first job for the service. When he asks why she does it, she says, "I have a daughter. She's seven years old. I need the money."

Young explains that she needs to quit the business and get out of town, and in what must surely be one of the worst moments of her

> *Stacey removes her panties and stands naked, Jason says in his contrived accent, "I love America, I love America."*

life — busted naked soliciting sex on national television — she gives the impression that's exactly what she intends to do.

But who knows where she'll go, or if indeed this will be an episode that redirects her life. Where else . . . and how else . . . can she make five hundred dollars for one hour of work?

Sheriff Bill Young, Sheriff of Clark County, spring 2003: The prostitution and escort service business today is a huge industry in Las Vegas, as big as I've ever seen it, and I grew up here. I'd estimate it generates hundreds of millions of dollars in gross revenues. And from a police perspective, it is almost impossible to stop from the lowest rung on up. Part of the reason is that soliciting for prostitution is just a misdemeanor crime, and so we may spend a lot of tax dollars to set up a sting and then the girl is out on bail two hours later.

> ## *"I'd estimate it generates hundreds of millions of dollars in gross revenues."*
>
> – SHERIFF BILL YOUNG

Even to do a room sting for one of the outcall services is extremely time-consuming and expensive. Sometimes the hotel will comp us the rooms on either side of the room where the bust is set up, but most of the time the hotels don't want us there, so we have to pay for the rooms. In a typical operation you have four or five detectives assigned to do it right, and you have to make fake ID, which is time consuming, and you have to make a fictitious out-of-state driver's license that looks legit with a name that's never been used, and you have to buy a legit plane ticket because the working girl wants to see that you recently flew in, and you have to pack a suitcase to make it look like you've been living in the hotel room for a few days. A lot of

Chapter 8

time and money goes into making the officer look like an honest to goodness tourist out for a good time.

The whole operation is done not just to get the prostitute, but also to get the guys running the whole operation, but it is very difficult, because they have a call-alert system in their industry and they close ranks when we go after them. When a girl goes to a hotel room she calls in to the service and tells them her location and that she's on the clock. Her business usually takes her just 20 to 30 minutes, so if she doesn't call back in about half an hour and report in, the service knows she's been busted. Even though these competing businesses hate each other, they all unite when there's a bust and call one another and report that the room in that hotel is no good. You might get two or three girls at most in one of these sting operations, and you spend a ton of police resources doing it. Meanwhile the girl gets no jail time and pays a small bail fee and is out working again the same night. So ultimately, in vice you are more productive working the girls who are freelancing at the bars and nightclubs, and you work the pimps and you work the streets.

Ultimately, you're just chasing your tail, but you have to keep the pressure on them because the whole industry is perfect for racketeering. I am hopeful that the new unit at the FBI in Las Vegas might take a look at it and work with us on creating a federal case against these bigger operators. It's a classic RICO situation. Roughly defined, racketeering occurs whenever you have a group of people that orchestrate a business for the practice of committing crimes. I think there are a lot of organized crime people behind these prostitution services, and there are international organized crime forces at work as well. And there are high-level pimps who place these girls in these services because it is relatively low risk and high profit. Those are the guys we want to stop.

The last few years in Las Vegas there has been a lot of influx in street prostitution. There was a time when there was a ton of street prostitution both downtown and on the Strip. But then when Sheriff John Moran was elected [1982], he promised to clean up the streets, so a lot of that business moved inside. And the Strip properties liked that better.

And then the street business mostly occurred downtown, on South Paradise between Flamingo and Tropicana, and a little out on Boulder Highway. So we had to prioritize our manpower because we have only about 25 detectives permanently assigned to vice. That is not a huge contingent considering the type of sexually oriented crimes we have here and the growing number of hotels. So now we spend about 50 percent of our time fighting street prostitution primarily in the downtown area, and 50 percent on the Strip in the higher end prostitution — meaning the call girls working independently at the bars, working through the bell desks, and working with the on-call services. Then of course in between all of that we have an active team that works the pimps, and we've even had to focus on one more thing, and that is the prevalence of the pimps who are bringing juvenile girls here.

Detective Brian Evans, Metro Vice Unit: In 1995 we started Operation Stop, to reduce the number of child prostitutes. The average age of these girls that come to town is 15. I've seen them as young as 11 or 12. They are primarily white girls.

The pimp hooks them on emotional dependency. He convinces the girl he is her one friend, her best friend, her lover, and her only source of support. Normally the girl is extremely vulnerable because she has been sexually abused by a family member or family friend. Drugs and alcohol are frequently a factor in the dependency on the pimp, but not always. Seventy-five percent of them are working out of hotels. They are recruited in other cities and brought here because there is so much more money to be made here than in San Francisco or L.A.

"Michael," Las Vegas Undercover Law Enforcement Agent: Pimps like 15-year-old girls for many reasons: they are easy to control, for one. And they can make more money with them because the girl has less mileage on her and therefore can command a higher dollar fee. A pimp once told me that johns don't like a woman who has more mileage on her than an eight-track tape. Also, if a pimp puts five young girls in a room together they form an alliance and look out for one another. They tend to be more loyal. The older hooker might be inclined to dangle her stuff for another pimp, try to leverage herself to get a better deal. Plus, the young girl has no kids and is likely to stay more faithful to the pimp because she has no one else on her side.

> *"The average age of these girls that come to town is 15. I've seen them as young as 11 or 12. They are primarily white girls."*
>
> — Detective Brian Evans

Sheriff Young: It's a sign of the sickness in our world that the younger the girl is, the higher price she fetches. In some countries and some cultures, for example in Canada and some countries in Europe, a prostitute that is over 17 is too old to work and so they come to the States. We are sadly seeing more and more young girls. My last experience when I was working vice was that a 15-year-old girl could command from $500 to $1,000, more than the average 25-year-old woman.

It seems for some reason that most of the American girls that come to Las Vegas to hook are from the Midwest. It's hard to fathom why, but if you were to survey prostitutes across the country, I would bet the number-one city that they come from is Minneapolis. That city seems to draw a lot of wayward girls from small towns in the Midwest, and so it's a fertile recruiting ground for pimps who flood in from New York City, Detroit, and Chicago. They find these girls from small towns who want out of their present lives. So you get the girl who wanted to break away from Waterloo, Iowa, going to Minneapolis, and then being taken wherever.

> "It's a sign of the sickness in our world that the younger the girl is, the higher price she fetches."
>
> – SHERIFF YOUNG

Brian Evans: I've seen a lot of girls coming in from the Pacific Northwest recently, the Seattle and Portland areas. A lot of them are runaways and pot smokers. The pimp is usually from another big city, and he'll go into these towns and recruit these girls and bring them to Las Vegas, because this is where the big action is.

The pimp will get a string of girls, and take all the money that's earned and dole it out to them as he sees fit. The "bottom bitch" is the pimp's main girl, the one with the most experience, and she will frequently break in the new girls. Her incentive is that if she can get the young girl making money then she won't have to work as hard. But she'll eventually be replaced. The young girl's incentive is to replace the bottom bitch and improve her status. So they're in competition with each other. The pimp always wants his girls competing to win his favor. He might have the bottom bitch living with him, and three or four girls in a Budget Suites hoping to improve their status and move up to the house with him. It's a very insulated, narrowly focused existence for the girls. They just don't see themselves as having other options.

Here's a story you might find hard to believe. I knew a woman who had an MBA from Harvard. She had a relationship with a casino host, and later found out he was married. A pimp overheard her on a phone conversation saying that she hated to see the relationship end because they'd had great sex. The pimp started talking to her about all the money she could make in Las Vegas and before long she started hooking. Now this is an intelligent, highly educated woman we're talking about here. Once she started making money he demanded she give him a big cut. Then he held her against her will and made her fax in her resignation as a hospital administration worker. Some time later he and his friends had what

> ## "They just don't see themselves as having other options."
>
> – Detective Brian Evans

they call a "pimp party" on her. They beat her up, urinated on her, and defecated on her in a parking lot, just to let her know that she couldn't freelance in this town. It was all about humiliating her as a way of maintaining control over her.

We try to bust these scumbags and go for asset forfeiture, where we take all their valuables so they have nothing to show their recruits. A pimp has two things: what they call Front and Clout. Front is how he looks. Clout is his shtick, the business he can portray, his standing in the game, his material possessions. Our job is to take away his Front and his Clout.

"Michael": There is one pimp in town who shows girls his Clout right away. He has a nice house and he takes them there and basically flashes the glorified street life. He does the father figure-protector stuff with them, trying to get that dependency started. But he also uses big-time intimidation. This guy's deal is to show the new girls pictures of girls that are dead — whether they are actually dead bodies or just girls pretending to be dead is up for debate — but the straight-on message is that if the girl doesn't work hard for him and do what she's told she'll end up like the girls in the pictures. We've busted this dude a few times and he's done some jail time, but he's out now and back in business.

Sheriff Young: In my opinion, there's not as much prostitution being arranged through the bell desks as there was years ago. There was a big bell desk bust in one of the major hotels in the 1980s [the Las Vegas Hilton] that got a lot of media attention, but now something like that wouldn't draw much attention because it's not a violent crime. I think it's reduced because the hotels are now part of a larger corporate structure. For years, at places like the Desert Inn and the Stardust, the Dunes and the Aladdin, the bellmen would make the better part of their living by supplying girls for customers. It was pretty big money for them. But then corporate America came into Las Vegas and companies like Park Place, Harrah's, and MGM became big players here in town and the bell desks got less active in procuring girls. I noticed the slowdown mostly around 1990 when The Mirage opened and they would not tolerate it and they hired a lot of female bell girls. That was obviously a deterrent to a customer asking where he could find a girl. A man is just not going to seek that kind of information from a woman employee. So that changed the dynamic too.

"Michael": The sex industry thrives in Las Vegas through a network of service workers whose livelihood depends on tips. This is not an indictment of these people; it's just a fact of life that someone working hard for his family in a hotel environment is going to be responsive to big tippers. From bartenders to cocktail waitresses to valet parkers to bellmen to limo and cab drivers, big tips will go a long way with these people, because it's these workers who have the closest contact with the tourists who bring millions of dollars of discretionary entertainment income to town. So if an older widowed woman inquires of a bartender where she might find male companionship and tokes him with a twenty, the odds are pretty good that the bartender can hook her up with a male escort, or gigolo. Same thing with a man in town for a convention who is looking for a hooker. If he's a good tipper, he's going to get that information pretty quickly, because the bartender may get a cut of the action from the hooker he calls with the lead.

> *"The sex industry thrives in Las Vegas through a network of service workers whose livelihood depends on tips."*
>
> —MICHAEL

Brian Evans: There's more hookers in town now than ever before, by a mile. When I worked vice in 1989, I might go into a Strip hotel and see three girls, and I knew two of them. At any given time I can go into a hotel now and see 10 to 15 hanging out. And there might be another 10 floating around that I don't see or couldn't tell what they are up to.

Sheriff Young: I've heard there are some independent madams in town who have top-dollar girls. There could be half a dozen by now. When I was in vice from 1988 through '95 there were two or three. I remember there was one girl, who has since died, who was part of the Heidi Fleiss ring. Heidi was a franchisee of a big prostitution ring that emanated out of Miami. We busted the ring here at the MGM Grand in 1994 when I was running the vice squad and there were local girls attached to it. But they didn't have enough girls for this particular party so they flew some of Heidi's girls in from L.A. We actually met them at the airport. We drove the limousine that picked them up and they showed up with boxes of Cuban cigars to give their clients. They thought they were going to make 'bank' in two days at this big executive party in a luxury suite at the Grand. We ended up busting the girl that Charlie Sheen had written $55,000 in checks to. She was part of Heidi's ring. Heidi was in jail at the time, but somebody was trying to keep her operation going with her girls.

> *"If you scrape back enough layers of mud, you'll usually find a pimp."*
>
> – SHERIFF YOUNG

There are today lots of rings and little pockets and cells of activity in prostitution. But in most cases there are males behind it. If you scrape back enough layers of mud, you'll usually find a pimp.

"Michael": I had the opportunity early in my career to work vice, but I passed on it. I'd seen it in my extended family and my neighborhood growing up, and I just find it so dirty. I don't look at prostitution as a victimless crime. You can say it's being done at the top levels by consenting adults, but there is venereal disease passed from the cheating husband to his wife, and sometimes on to unborn children. So they become victims of it. And the IRS isn't getting their share of that revenue, and the state of Nevada isn't getting its share. And at the lowest levels of course it's the underprivileged or uneducated girl who finds herself the victim of some slick pimp.

Sheriff Young: What I would like to do is go after the ownership of these prostitution businesses and nail the people who are making the really big bucks in this industry, but the resources are not on our side. We are not going to get it done from the bottom up. We have to work it from the top down. Some of these organizations are in Las Vegas, and some aren't, although I think most of it is here now. They are making huge money, and they watch their money very carefully. These entertainment service guys live like rock stars. They are making hundreds and hundreds of thousands of dollar each year and hiding it. They are not paying taxes on most of it, they have unlimited sex, they live the great life. They don't really work, other than to set up these scams.

Brian Evans: Most of the street pimps are black, but most of the guys running the outcall services are white. A while back one of these guys had a secretary delivering a bag of money to the bank and she got rolled in the parking lot. Three guys rolled her outside, and they got $150,000 from the weekend earnings. That's a pretty good take for one weekend.

Sheriff Young: The guys who run these services have all sorts of First Amendment protections to hide behind, and there's no prosecution on it anyway. If someone goes to jail it's usually the girls and not the owners, so the monetary reward far outweighs the risks. It is very difficult to pin a pandering rap on these outcall owners. Outcall dancing has been found by the Supreme Court to bear Constitutional muster as an art form. So unless you have a recorded conversation or a videotape or a tremendous amount of corroborating evidence to show that the owner expects the girl to go out there and work as a prostitute, he claims he is just getting the $150 service fee for the girl showing up at the room to dance. And the way it works is that he keeps the entire fee. She works on tips or anything else she's willing to do for the client. Do the math. If the owner gets a $150 service fee from 30 or 40 girls who go out there three or four times a night, he's making well over $10,000 a night. Where it gets fuzzy is how much of the "tip" money the owner decides to keep. The ones that get greedy will occasionally get snitched out by the girls.

As I said, it's a tough thing to prove, and that's why the way to stop it is through the Feds and racketeering charges. Federal law enforcement has the laws and the resources to go after it the right way, but it's awfully difficult on a local level.

> "Outcall dancing has been found by the Supreme Court to bear Constitutional muster as an art form."
>
> – Sheriff Young

Brian Evans: The way I understand it, if the outcall service charges the customer $150 up front, $125 of that goes to the service, $15 to the girl who took the phone call and made the appointment, and $10 to the dancer. It's then up to the dancer to hustle tips from there. But those girls are wary of the customer. They want to see ID, airplane tickets, room receipts; they'll snoop in the bathroom looking in your shaving kit. And most of them have pimps as well, so they don't want to get busted because it will piss off their pimp. It's a tricky game.

"Michael": You'd be surprised at how much prostitution takes place outside these gentlemen's clubs. The game for a girl dancing in one of these clubs is to size you up as a customer, and see just how much money she can get out of you. The game for the customer is to see how much he can get from the girl without spending his whole wad. I know for a fact that a lot of these girls are doing tricks in the back of limousines. The driver gets a hundred dollar tip for driving around while they're doing their thing in the limo. It beats having to go back to a hotel. You have your own little room right there in the limo. Like I said, the people in the service jobs have all sorts of ways of making money off the sex industry.

Sheriff Young: I have not been in a topless joint since I left vice in '95. I try to stay as far away from that industry as possible. I know there is some prostitution going on from there. How much I don't know. The girls make a lot of money just dancing there, but there are girls that get greedy, or are not making money that week, and they'll make it any way they can, with the right guy.

They might pick up a regular that they have gotten to know can't possibly be a police officer because he spent more than $20. The dancers know we have limited resources. But if a guy is coming in every night and he's a big tipper and he's spending $400 a night on lap dances, they know he's not a cop. If he's over 50 years old, they know he's not a cop. There are a lot of telltale signs. But if they develop a comfort level and can pick up another $500 or a grand with a regular customer, they'll do it.

But by no means am I saying that all these girls are hookers. A lot of them just dance, and won't do prostitution.

Brian Evans: I love my job because it's a challenge to beat the pimps at their own game, and it's so satisfying when you can get girls who are in bad situations to roll over and give up their pimps. We've turned around well over 500 girls since 1995, either got them out of the biz or out of town. And it's a good feeling when you can help someone pull out of the gutter.

"Michael:" When something gradually increases year after year, and you're right in the middle of it, you sometimes lose perspective. But this city's sex industry has gone crazy in the last few years. People who haven't been to town in seven or eight years, and thought Las Vegas was still trying to be a family-oriented destination, are shocked by what they see. When you see a billboard of a sexy woman with her legs apart that says "Direct to your Room," and it gives a phone number, and it's located right on Flamingo Avenue in front of the Rio Hotel, that's shocking to a lot of people. Those of us who live here and see it every day get numb to it after awhile, at least until our children in the back seat ask us, "Daddy, what's that lady doing?"

> *"It could be that many people still think prostitution is legal in Clark County . . ."*
>
> –SHERIFF YOUNG

Sheriff Young: It could be that many people still think prostitution is legal in Clark County, but from a law enforcement position I will tell you that we have tried to exorcise that business from the community with legal means. It would seem that it is something that you could legislate against easily, but every law ever crafted to prevent prostitution has been struck down, whether it be the handouts that advertise the girls direct to your room, the right to distribute literature, or the right to dance as an art form. What it finally comes down to is that it is a waste of your resources to pursue these things when they are not going to be upheld in the courts.

It just needs to be addressed from the top down, with Federal resources, because of the laws that are clearly being violated. They are transporting people across state lines for the purposes of prostitution, they are not paying taxes on the money, there are a lot of drugs

Chapter 8

involved in the business, there are children under 18 working in the industry, and on and on.

Would it be detrimental to Las Vegas to wipe out prostitution? No, I don't think so. There is still plenty of other adult entertainment here. I am just not a big fan of prostitution.

The Gold Dust Twins

"It is as if all the hip young suburban gals of America named Lana, Deborah, and Sandra, who gather wherever the arc lights shine and the studs steady their coiffures in the plate-glass reflection, have convened in Las Vegas with their bouffant hair above and anatomically stretch-pant-swathed little bottoms below, here on the new American frontier."

— TOM WOLFE,

*THE KANDY*KOLORED TANGERINE*FLAKE STREAMLINE BABY*

You may have seen them strolling past the blackjack tables, or using the correct fork in the fancier gourmet restaurants in the upscale hotels on the Strip. Places like The Mirage and the Venetian, New York-New York and the Bellagio, Mandalay Bay and Caesars Palace. Women look twice and admire how pretty they are, or take note of their fashion sense. The look most men give them can be spelled with three letters: W-O-W!

These two stunning women, both blonde, both near 30 but appearing five years younger, look like professional models, or perhaps aspiring actresses. They are the sort of creatures that win beauty pageants and would be out of the dating reach of the average guy, who would logically assume that women this attractive are to be seen and not touched. But that's where the man is mistaken.

These women, and we've agreed to call them Brenda and Lexy for the purposes of confidentiality, will definitely date. But usually only an hour at a time, and they are anything but cheap. Try five hundred dollars and up. And the clock is always ticking.

How they ended up at this point in their lives in Las Vegas, plying the world's oldest profession, comprises two distinctly different tales. One came here with no idea what she was about to get into; the other had it in the back of her mind all along.

Brenda and Lexy are good friends, and they often work together, either from contacts they have gotten from their madam/business manager Karin, whom we met earlier, or on a freelance basis. Karin gets $1,000 an hour per girl when she schedules them, of which they get half plus any tips they receive. When they work alone, the sky is the limit. The take depends on two factors: how deep is the client's bankroll, and how hot is the blood pulsing through his veins when he sees the two of them stark naked. It's not uncommon for either

Brenda or Lexy to turn a one-night appointment with a man into a three-day excursion and make up to seven or eight thousand for their trouble.

Brenda earned over $17,000 on Super Bowl weekend alone this year, and two days after we interviewed Lexy she received over $20,000 in tips from some high-stakes craps players when she got on an incredible roll, held the dice for 45 minutes, and earned them about $300,000 from her hot hand. When she told me about it later, she joked, "Normally I just get three hundred for a hand job. That's by far the most money I've ever made with my clothes on."

B renda: She's 28, from the Midwest, with a degree in English literature from a Big Ten University. She bears a striking resemblance to Sarah Jessica Parker, the star of *Sex in the City*, but she is slightly taller and more slender. She has legs that the actress would kill for. But she's heard the comparison to Parker so often that it's become tiresome to her.

"Just the other day, a woman took my photograph in the airport and when I asked her why, she said she thought I might be her," she says, with a slight shrug of her shoulders as we talk over a meal in the Summerlin area.

Brenda explains that she came to Las Vegas 11 months ago with a man she was dating, but not long after they got here she discovered his real motivation was to live off her earnings. In effect, he had hustled her away from her tranquil home, out here to the desert, with a plan of pimping this beautiful young woman who had never before received money for sex. Once she realized his intentions, she ended the relationship.

"I guess the short answer was that I moved out here because of him," she says, teasing a salad and choosing her words carefully. "But behind the decision to come to Las Vegas was a sense of boredom with my life. I'd always lived in the same part of the country, and there was just too much predictability in my life. Every day was too much the same."

Brenda had held a job working with children for several years. It was a career she found both financially and emotionally satisfying, but she yearned for a different experience, one in which every day would bring a new adventure and put her more on the edge.

"I could see the hinges on Pandora's Box, and I wanted to see what was in there," she says. I find her allusion curious, and surprising, and I ask her to elaborate on it.

"I had definite prejudices about prostitution," she says. "But I was also intrigued by it. This man I was with knew a lot about that world, and I guess even though he angered me with it, he also provoked my curiosity."

Brenda writes every day in a journal, and tells me she's working on a novel based on her own life. That might in part explain why she chose her current occupation. There's no denying that her experiences as a woman of the night provide highly commercial subject matter, and she admits being part of my book may be a valuable learning experience.

Brenda had been in Las Vegas several times before, on short vacations. One time on a lark she went to Cheetah's and danced topless. She thought that might be a good way to make money for a while.

But she quit after two days. "I hated the fact that men could sit there and gawk at me naked without spending a dollar."

She says she had never before used her sexuality to get things from men. Her family was comfortable financially, and she had always made good money at her job. But she also knew that sex with an attractive woman like herself was something that men put great value on, and she wasn't greatly troubled by morality issues. She didn't think early on that her life would ever come to that, but she had at times pondered the possibility.

Brenda lost her virginity in high school, and says she was more sexually active in her teens than she was in college. Sadly, when she was just 16, an older brother, her only sibling, died of a heroin overdose. "It's something you never really recover from," she says. "It devastated me and made me hate drugs and how they can ruin a person's life."

> *"I hated the fact that men could sit there and gawk at me naked without spending a dollar."*
>
> —BRENDA

Yet she'll smoke a joint in the evenings to relax. She doesn't consider marijuana as addictive or damaging as alcohol, and she likes to write when she's stoned. "I live alone and do a lot of thinking these days," she says. "I'll admit I feel anxious in Las Vegas. I'm not in a real settled place in my soul right now. I get a little depressed when I have long spells between working because it gives me too much time to question what I'm doing. When I work a lot it keeps my adrenaline up because there's a real high to getting paid for sex. It gives me a great sense of power and control. It's hard to explain."

Karin had told me in an earlier interview that the attention and wealth that comes to a beautiful woman, who sells herself for big money, is extremely addictive. That rather than making a woman feel cheap, the act of sex for hire actually makes her feel expensive, and greatly valued. And a carefree lifestyle full of creature comforts, for which money is no object, is a hard habit to shake. It occurs to me as I talk with Brenda that she's underscoring that very point.

Karin says Brenda is at her best with large bachelor parties, doing a girl-girl show. "She becomes totally uninhibited," she says, "and feeds off the attention. She is a different person when she's up there and all eyes are on her. Yet there are times when I question whether she enjoys any part of it."

L exy: The first time I reach her by phone to request an interview she doesn't mince words. Five minutes into the conversation, she says, "A girlfriend once told me, 'Lexy, your pussy is lined with gold.' She said she'd never seen a girl who could get men to do whatever she wanted just by flicking her hair or winking at them.'

"And she told me that several years ago," Lexy says, "long before I moved to Las Vegas."

A stunning honey blonde with a deep tan and curvy figure, and with the richly textured New Joi-sy accent of a mob moll from the Soprano family, Lexy will tell you exactly how she feels. And she happens to feel, with apt justification, that she is the hottest little sex pistol on the block. She has known she was irresistible to men from the time she was in junior high school, back in New Jersey. "What man wouldn't want to be with me?" she says, flipping a swatch of hair back and laughing with the assurance of one who has been with plenty.

"Oh, honey, I was a naughty girl growing up," she says, seated at the kitchen table in the new custom home she's recently purchased in southwest Las Vegas. "I lost my virginity when I was 13, to a nay-ba-hood boy."

She recounts her experiences with glee, laughing at the memories the way you'd expect from a man boasting about his first sexual encounter. "I absolutely loved it the first time," she says. "The boy was a great fuck. And I ended up having regular sex with him and his friends."

With that she begins to apply moisturizer to her legs in a slow, methodical manner. She's such a natural tease that she's oblivious to how much this can distract an interviewer.

"Excuse me, but my legs are drying out," she says. "I've gotten too much sun in the last week. I spent three days in Beverly Hills, three days at Lake Las Vegas, and yesterday I was in San Francisco. My client and I were supposed to go to a Giants game and see Barry Bonds, but when he picked me up at the airport we went straight to the hotel and never left." She laughs and flicks her golden mane back over her shoulder. "Men can be so horny sometimes." She reaches into her purse and tosses the unused game tickets on the table to confirm her story.

"Ah, they were just playing the Pittsburgh Pirates," I say. "Not that big a deal."

Lexy developed faster than any of the other girls in her neighborhood, and she didn't attempt to hide her assets. "I was a 36 DD at age 16," she says. "I had the biggest, most beautiful boobs you've ever seen.

The Gold Dust Twins

Do you think I drove those boys nuts? There were all these gorgeous boys in my neighborhood, and by the time I finished high school I had been with nearly all of them."

Interviewing such a brazen vixen, and hearing her totally uninhibited stories of growing up as the easy girl in her neighborhood, is rather unsettling. It might be compared to the discomfort a woman must feel sitting through an Andrew Dice Clay concert. As Lexy shares her Marine barracks stories, I can't help reflecting on how sexually liberated she is. It's almost as though she were raised in a society that encouraged and rewarded young girls for being promiscuous. It's a distinctly different culture than the one I was raised in. I can't detect even a whisker of guilt or remorse in her.

"I had sex with over 100 men by the time I graduated from high school," she says. "Oh, yeah. And I loved it every time. I broke some hearts, let me tell you. So many of them wanted to fall in love with me and keep me for their steady girlfriend, but I just wanted the sex. I admit I was lucky as hell not to get pregnant, and I think the only thing I ever caught was chlamydia. I knew from the time I was 13 that I could pretty much control men with sex. And that's a nice power to have."

She admits that her popularity with boys worked in reverse with the girls in her school. "The girls didn't like the fact that I hung around with boys in the upper classes," she says. "They used to knock me for being pretty, like it was a bad thing and I should be sorry for it."

On five different occasions she says she actually got in fights with girls that were jealous of her.

Lexy's only roommates are four cats, and they stroll freely through her house — on my lap, over my notes, around the tape recorder.

Chapter 9

"Please excuse them," she says, "but they are allowed to do whatever they want here. It's their house as much as mine."

In recounting her decision to "turn pro," three years ago, she says it was something she'd always contemplated doing.

"I broke up with a boyfriend in 2000," she says. "I was completely faithful to him for the three years we lived together here. He was not faithful to me. That is why our relationship ended. I realized then that the time was right to give it a try, to see if in fact my pussy *was* lined with gold. But I wanted to get into the business the right way. I knew I would never let a man live off my earnings. I think pimps are worthless and disgusting and I'm a big girl. I am very capable of taking care of myself. So I just took a flyer one day and responded to an ad in that little giveaway magazine *City Life*. I went to a house where I met a man who was running an escort service. He took one look at me and said, 'Whoa, you are going to make a lot of money.'"

The on-call owner was a man in his mid-30s that Lexy remembers as a gentleman. "He didn't try to screw me and he didn't even make me get naked," she says. "He was pretty new at the game, and I sensed he really didn't know how to run the business. But shortly after meeting him, like the next day, he called me and gave me a room number at Bally's. It was two men wanting two girls. The other girl was named Lisa. It was very weird because the guy I was with that very first time just kept telling me how beautiful I was, and he started crying as he was getting it on with me. The other girl was startled by it. He was actually sobbing and saying, 'You are the most beautiful thing I've ever seen.' He paid me a thousand dollars for 45 minutes, plus the two hundred for the service. Oh, and his name was John, which was kinda funny. My first john was a John."

She took a second job that same day, and ended up with another $700. And she made $1500 the second day. Two days of work had netted her $3200, enough to pay her apartment rent for three months. "Knowing that I had to grill the guys on my own to make any money was a real challenge," she says. "But I knew I could do it. I would do a slow strip, just down to a g-string, and then say, (*in a kewpie doll voice*) 'How much do you want it, Big Boy? Show me a little gratitude, and I'll show you some . . . If you're nice to me, I'll be *so-o* nice to you.' Then I might just slide my g-string over an inch and give him a little pussy peek to loosen up that wallet."

She laughs at the thought of just how easy it was.

> ## "Damn, I might as well have just picked their pockets, they were so helpless."
> —Lexy

"Damn, I might as well have just picked their pockets, they were so helpless. But of course I would never steal. I don't have to."

Karin says men love Lexy because "She's more sexual than a lot of other girls in the business. And she's absolutely sure of herself and her sexuality. Her parents must have given her a lot of love for her to have that kind of self-esteem. She knows she's hot, and I think that confidence is very appealing to her clients. She gets them thinking that they're buying the hottest piece of ass that ever lived."

Brenda and Lexy have worked together about 10 times, and on two different occasions have done girl-girl shows to get the party started. Brenda is far more at ease performing than Lexy. "I'm not

Chapter 9

sure that she's as comfortable with her body as I am," says Brenda. "She doesn't like to be the focus of attention of a lot of guys."

Lexy agrees, saying "If it's a big bachelor party with like 40 guys and a lot of fanfare, you won't see me doing a show. I'm the girl in the back giving lots of blowjobs and making money. I prefer one-on-one."

Neither has ever been arrested, or really even come close to getting in trouble on the job. Brenda says a cop tried to solicit her one time in a hotel but she knew instinctively he was a policeman. "I listened to his spiel and finally said, 'Thanks for the offer, but I think I'll go eat some doughnuts,' and I just walked away."

Lexy recalls a time when she had two different clients, both big-money boys, staying at the same Strip hotel. When the security guard spotted her coming down one elevator, and going up another, he cautioned her that she couldn't do that. "He wasn't going to make me leave the hotel," she says. "He just said that what I was doing looked bad. And I knew I was taking a chance, but it was an unusual circumstance. I think I made about $4,000 that night."

Brenda says she won't have sex with couples together, although there is some demand for that. Lexy has no hesitation. "Oh, baby," she says. "Yeah, I like that. One time this really cute guy approached me in a hotel. I had dropped something on the floor and he said, 'Did you lose something?' And we started talking and he mentioned that his girlfriend was upstairs waiting for him.

"And I said, 'Well you better get up there.'

"And he said, 'Well, she's hoping I'll bring a pretty girl back there for her, but she's never been with a woman. It's one of the reasons we came to Las Vegas, to try that.'

"I told him it was his lucky day, and when I got to the room there was this beautiful girl, about 24, lying naked on the couch. They had a huge suite that we could get to only through the private elevators. She was really nervous, but excited, and asked me if I'd have a couple shots of whiskey with her to calm her down. So I did, and honey, it was a great time. I tore both of them up. They have since become regular customers of mine."

It was funny listening to each of them talk about the fashion sense of the other.

"I have to tell Brenda to tone down her dress sometimes," says Lexy. "Sometimes when we go to the hotels she dresses a little too much like a hooker. Her skirts can get a little short and draw too much attention."

Without having heard Lexy's critique, Brenda tells me, "There are times that Lexy dresses like a porn star, with all the hair and the tits pushed way up. But then a lot of guys like that bad-girl look."

When I tell Karin what the girls have said about each other, she laughs heartily. "Oh, that's too funny," she says. "Here they are working together as great partners and dissing each other on the sly."

But it's clear that the two women, so different in so many ways, truly like each other.

"Brenda is a beautiful girl," says Lexy. "She is smart and sweet and gives really good head."

"For some reason, those three attributes don't seem to belong in the same list," I say, but Lexy just keeps rolling.

"I think Brenda has the best ass and legs in the business. And she has her college degree, you know. We're quite a bit different, but I consider her a good friend. I doubt if either one of us will be doing this two years from now. I know I'll be married by then and she probably will be, too."

"You sound very certain of that," I say.

"Oh, there's no doubt," she says. "I have a lot of guys that want to marry me right now. My clients are always telling me that I'm the type of girl they could take home to Mama. Of course, it would be good if Mama never found out what Lexy has been doing in Las Vegas."

"Would you ever marry a client?" I ask. Her immediate response sounds like a bit out of Abbott and Costello.

"When I find the right guy I don't want him to be a trick," she says, "because I don't want a guy like that who's picking up a girl like me because he doesn't need to know that I'm a girl like me but I'll always know he's a guy like that because he picked me up."

When I ask her if she can repeat that, because I got lost in my note taking, she repeats the same riddle verbatim.

⟨≋⟩

Brenda: "I actually met Karin through the guy I was dating," she says. "I won't tell you how. The first professional job I did was at Mandalay Bay. It was a bachelor party with five girls and maybe 15 guys. It was a fairly calm crowd. I didn't even do a lap dance or anything. I was just there sort of as eye candy. I made $400 that night, and I enjoyed being around the other girls. Two of them did a girl/girl show, so I got to see what that was all about. I thought it was pretty cool, but I wasn't sure at that point whether I could ever do that."

Because Karin wanted Brenda to learn the ropes quickly and start earning good money, Karin started calling her regularly, and giving her more advanced jobs each time. On her next call Brenda was required just to give the man oral sex. Once again, she made $400.

She says she didn't dwell too much on what she was doing that evening. "I just wanted to get through it, to see if I could do it. And I did," she says. "The man was nice. He wanted a blow job without a condom, but I wouldn't do it and he didn't make an issue of it."

On her next job, she was asked to participate in a girl/girl show. Brenda asked the other girl to take the lead, and she followed along. They used a double-headed dildo and simulated being totally turned on to each other. This is standard practice in a bachelor party situation, and it makes the girls' jobs much easier when they pair off with the men, because the vast majority of men love to watch women together. The show is often the only foreplay required. "Most men come in about five or 10 minutes," she says. "But if drugs or alcohol are involved it's a different story. The worst ones are the guys who use cocaine. It's annoying. They can never come. But they have to pay anyway.

> "The worst are guys who use cocaine. They can never come. But they have to pay anyway."
>
> —BRENDA

"I learned that men are absolutely stupefied when they see girls playing with each other's pussies," says Brenda. "It's so odd. It's like someone has surgically removed their brains when they see it."

"I was good at the shows," she adds. "The other girl said I adapted so quickly she couldn't believe I hadn't done it before. From that point on, I would always be involved in the girl/girl show at the beginning."

Brenda got a lot of work in the beginning from Karin, but she quickly learned that's the pattern. The new girls get most of the jobs. So she started freelancing, working the hotels, paying close attention to the conventions in town by referencing the Internet, learning the ropes.

"I liked that by working on my own I could keep whatever I got," she says. "And the art of negotiating was something I got pretty good at. But I felt safer when I went out with another girl. Even if we split up and don't do a job together, at least there's another person who knows where you're going. I had a lot of nights where I would make like two thousand dollars for three hours with a guy. That pays a lot of my overhead right there. And it gives me the freedom to leave town and clear my head whenever I need it. I like to just take off for Jamaica and totally chill out."

Less than a year from starting her new profession, Brenda says she now gets only about 20 percent of her jobs through Karin.

"Brenda doesn't have her heart quite in it anymore," says Karin in a subsequent interview. "She's lost some of the momentum she had early on, but I understand. I'd be surprised if she's still doing this a year from now. She's just going through a transition period in her life."

Lexy: "I met Karin coming out of the Bellagio one night about a year ago. She looked great, and I told her so," she says. "I asked her where she was coming from and she said, 'Oh, a client.' And I said, 'Well, I hope you had a better night than me.' We just started talking and she told me she ran an adult entertainment business, and it started right there. After you've been doing this awhile, there's sort of an unspoken knowledge you have about which girls are working girls."

Lexy's method isn't complicated. It doesn't have to be when you look like her. Although Brenda might disagree, Lexy says she dresses down when she goes to the nice hotels. "I want to look like a businesswoman enjoying myself, or the wife or girlfriend of a hotel guest," she says.

And she knows precisely what she's looking for when she makes her first pass through the casino. Basically, it's a well-dressed and well-groomed man in his 40s or 50s. She looks at the shoes, and the watch. If he's wearing a custom suit, she can identify the designer. If it's Brioni, that's a sure thing.

> *She knows precisely what she's looking for when she makes her pass through the casino.*

She avoids younger, hipper hotels like the Hard Rock and the Palms.

"At that center bar at the Hard Rock, there's all sorts of good looking girls in town looking to get laid for free," she says. "And the young guys who hang out there don't have the cash. That's not what I'm after."

Often, she'll sit next to a potential client and start playing blackjack, but only if it's a $25 minimum. She's even played the $100 tables, but that's risky because she might lose a lot of her own money and not score a trick. Any man with a normal measure of heterosexual desire will engage her in conversation soon after she's taken a seat. Within five or 10 minutes the small talk will lead to the thousand-dollar question: What do you do?

"At that point," she says, "I will toss my hair back, cock my head, look the man dead in the eye and say in a barely audible whisper, 'I give erotic massages. Would you like one?'"

Oftentimes, the man will scoop up his chips immediately and they'll head upstairs. Of course, there's always the possibility that his wife is somewhere in the hotel, or that he's not staying at that property, in which case other arrangements might be made or the deal might be scotched.

"But if it doesn't happen with the first guy, by that time I've usually gotten some other man's attention," Lexy says. "I never get shut out completely, Honey. There are times when I'll see a man walking behind the table, just waiting for the right moment to make his move. And if the first guy doesn't take the bait, the second guy will jump right in."

Lexy estimates that 75 percent of her clients are married and says she prefers that because "all of the single guys want to date me, and I'm not interested in dating a guy who pays for girls like me."

She says one guy wanted to date her with the condition that she keep on working. "He wanted to hear about all the tricks I was turning," she says. "But that had the smell of a pimp all over it. I think he was a sicko."

When pimps do approach her, as occasionally happens, she ignores them and walks by.

"When a black pimp tries to talk to me, and tell me what he can do for me, I say, 'Yeah, I know what you can do for me. You can sit your fat black ass on the couch so I can go out and work my ass off to bring you money.'

"They realize right away that they don't want any part of me. I just think pimps are so worthless. But it's not a racial thing with me. I have a big party coming up this weekend with a bunch of NFL players, all black guys and real gentlemen. It will be several other girls and me, for a 3-6-9 deal."

I ask her to explain the numbers.

"That's three hundred for a hand job, six hundred for a BJ, and nine hundred for full sex," she says. "It should be a great time."

What do most men want for their money? I ask.

"Ninety percent of the guys want to go down on me," she says, without blinking. "I have a shaved pussy and when they see that they go absolutely nuts. You know the guy's wife doesn't have that, and he's just got to have it. And nearly all the married men want blowjobs. Maybe it's because they don't get head at home. They don't want the mother of their children sucking dick. Who knows?"

The men who want anal sex are out of luck.

"I don't do butt," she says. "They can lick it; they just can't stick it."

When I tell Karin about my conversation with Lexy, she says, "Is she a character or what? You can see why men get such a kick out of her. They are never disappointed with that girl. They know they're going to get good sex and a lot of laughs along with it."

Brenda: "I don't know how long I'll be here," she says. "Maybe a couple years, I'm not sure. This has been a crazy year. If you'd told me two years ago that this year I'd be in Las Vegas doing this I never would have believed you. I don't like leading this double life. My parents think I'm a convention hostess."

Brenda says she wants to get married sometime in the next few years, but she doesn't buy into the *Pretty Woman* fantasy of a customer sweeping her off her feet and taking her away from it all. "You know the Richard Gere character would throw his pretty woman's past back in her face at some point in the future," she says. "That's pure Hollywood. I would want a man to find me on another level, with a meeting of the minds. And I don't think it would be necessary for him to know about this phase of my life."

Lexy: "With what I'm doing right now I walk quickly into a guy's life and light it up for an hour or a day and then I walk out just as quickly. I know what I'm looking for in a husband. I want a guy who's never been married and doesn't have children, because I want to start with a clean slate. And he has to have a good-paying job to keep me in the style to which I've been accustomed. I also don't plan on telling him anything about this time in my life, because I know he'll have some past secrets he won't want to share with me and I won't press him on it. Hey, people can say what they want. I'm just using my natural gifts and talents to make good money and have some fun. Nobody's getting hurt here. It hasn't changed who I am as a person one single bit."

Lexy's parents also have no idea about her profession. "They think I work in sales with the conventions. And that I do some modeling, which I actually do. I'm registered with some agencies, and I'll do the hostess thing for a day or two at a convention, but of course when I talk to the customers and they start getting friendly I'll let them know about my other job. I get a lot of my clients that way. Plus it's a good cover."

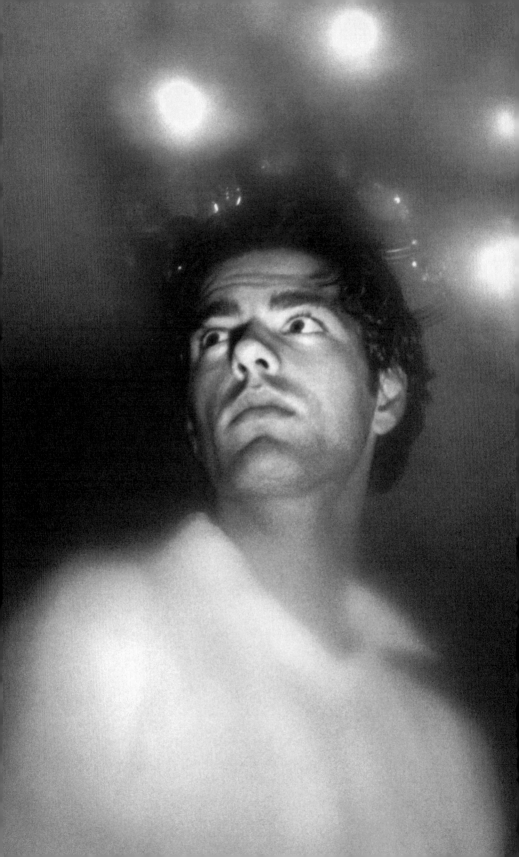

Where the Boys Are

"I think heaven has sent
you here, Dirk Diggler."

— JACK HORNER (BURT REYNOLDS) IN *BOOGIE NIGHTS*

I n the interest of being an equal opportunity reporter, I decided we needed to learn something about the male skin trade in Las Vegas. I had been told by an undercover Metro cop named "Michael" that there is a small contingent of male prostitutes in Las Vegas, midnight cowboys if you will, who make their living selling sex to both females and males looking for companionship.

But I found that these guys are tougher to expose to the light than the Russian Mafia. Every time I got close to an interview with someone I had been told was a brother in this fringe fraternity, he would disappear.

There was the man who calls himself "Sin," whose cell phone was permanently on voice mail. Twice when I called and explained my business, he returned the calls, but both times at odd hours of the night when he figured I wouldn't pick up the line. He left the message that he was willing to talk, but after I'd made several more return calls and e-mails, it became obvious that he only liked talking into recorders. No luck there.

And then there was the porn star named Alec, who when contacted by e-mail returned a note within the hour saying, "Okay, Buddy, I will try to call you." Try as he might, Alec never was able to complete the call.

Then there were two different friends of a friend who said they would be happy to talk to me about their profession, but then ducked and ran at the appointed time. Another man named Stephan told me he was thinking of writing his own book about hustling, but the next week he called to say he was retiring from the profession. The reason? He was getting married. Hmmm.

I wondered whether the only way to get an interview with a male prostitute was to leave a message saying something like, "Hi, I'm Jack, and I'm hornier than a two-peckered goat. You gotta help me out here. See, I just hit MegaBucks for seventeen million dollars and it's had the effect on my body of taking six Viagra with a chaser of oyster juice. The money is burning a hole in my pocket. Please call immediately so you can relieve me in more ways than one."

I finally landed an interview on the subject after I was told by a fellow journalist that he knew a man in town who had been a Chippendales-type dancer in a former nightclub called Bogey's. It was my associate's understanding that this fellow was the perfect source for my chapter on male entertainment — that he had worked as both a dancer and an escort. It turns out that while Javier was very knowledgeable about the business, he had never performed sex directly for money (although that became a question of semantics). Nevertheless, he provided a good starting point for my research into the other side of the fence.

Javier is a handsome man, lean and muscular, in his mid-40s. He's Puerto Rican by birth but moved to the U.S. as an infant and bears just the slightest hint of an accent. He has a gentle and sincere manner and was totally cooperative, even calling me back several times after the initial interview to answer follow-up questions.

Javier worked as a stripper for several years. His initial foray into adult entertainment came at Bogey's, the first Las Vegas club to present an all-male revue and host those frenzied spectacles called "Ladies Night" specials. Later on he danced at Olympic Gardens, in a sequestered section in the back of the building far better known as a gentlemen's club.

Currently retired from dancing and now working behind the scenes in the film industry, Javier can't hide a big smile when he reminisces about his years "shakin' the bacon."

"I was hired at Bogey's as one of a small contingent of bodybuilders who initially just walked around in Speedos and flexed our muscles for the women," he says. "But what a smorgasbord for a young guy who loved women. It was like a buffet every night. We had our pick of the ladies. I had just lost my virginity the year before I started there, so you can imagine how excited I was to go to work each night. I guess for the women it was just the novelty and newness of being able to stick money in a man's g-string that put them over the edge.

> ## "It was like a buffet every night."
>
> –JAVIER

We were getting blowjobs in the parking lots on our breaks, and there were frequent orgies, three guys and three girls, all swapping. It was right before AIDS broke out, so everyone was pretty fearless about the consequences."

Javier says the money was an afterthought. He was paid a mere twenty dollars a night plus tips, but he would have worked there for free. "I was basically a sexaholic in those days, so for me it was all about unlimited sex," he says. Javier recalls the only thing that surprised him was how the women would scream and yell and paw at guys who were obviously gay. "It created some awkward situations," he says. "A bunch of us would end up in a room and the gay guys would eventually excuse themselves. I was always surprised at how slow the women were to pick up on that."

He says the female customers he met told him they found it tremendously liberating to watch a show where they could turn the tables and treat men like pieces of meat. "I would have sex in the

Chapter 10

parking lot with a girl and she wouldn't even know my name," he says.

"There were women who would come to Las Vegas for a convention, or whatever, which in itself is kind of a liberating experience where they feel they can do whatever their libidos desire, and then to top it off by watching men strip for them, it just seemed to peel away whatever was left of their inhibitions."

One time a man from Canada asked Javier to have sex with his sister, who was a virgin. "The guy rented a hotel room for us and it was great," he says. "Obviously, when the guy took his sister into Bogey's that night that was his intention all along, to find a man to break her in. I was more than happy that he chose me to do the honors."

The strangest incident Javier recalls is the night he was approached by a well-dressed gentleman in the men's room as he stood at a urinal. "This guy had a deep southern accent — turns out he was from Mississippi — and he said, 'Your show is really great.'

"My first thought of course was that he was hitting on me. But then he said, 'Listen, my wife's out there and she loves black guys. I'd love for you to fuck her. Can you come back to the Hilton with us?' He handed me a hundred-dollar bill."

Javier left with them and once in the hotel room, the woman went into a bathroom and changed into a sexy negligee. When she returned, Javier said the man's demeanor dramatically changed. "He got this wild look in his eye and said, "I want you to fuck this white pussy like there's no tomorrow."

When I mention to Javier that this sounds like a scene right out of the movie *American Gigolo*, he agrees. "Yeah, that might be where the guy got the line," he says. "But I was young and dumb and the way I looked at it was that I was getting paid to have sex with a beautiful woman. The guy sat in a chair nearby. He was snorting cocaine and masturbating and saying, 'Fuck her, fuck her with that big black dick.' When it was over I felt sorry for her. We went at it for about five hours. My joint looked like a Hormel's skinless wiener."

Javier says that the next day the incident bothered his conscience, and he started going to church to pray about it. "I am a spiritual person," he says, "and I have great respect for people's feelings, but I was just consumed by sex back then. It can be an addiction.

"The man contacted me later and wanted me to find more black guys for her," he says. "This was a couple from the Deep South, a hotbed of racism, and this was the ultimate taboo for them. It was their fantasy. But I found it troubling."

Javier says that when he worked years later at the Olympic Gardens, there was far more competition among the male dancers. "It was all about hustling," he says. "Some guys would make $1500 a night there. As soon as a woman walked in, guys would be all over her to do a table dance, and some would do it for ten dollars. There were definitely tricks being done out of there. I was always hearing guys talk about their sugar mamas who would take care of them, or what wild action was going to happen later that night, after work. Although we were technically not allowed to date the customers, guys would meet the women at casinos later on and hook up."

> "... the way I looked at it was that I was getting paid to have sex with a beautiful woman."
>
> –JAVIER

He says the general age range of the patrons was between 27 and 45. "The best tippers were women with professional careers who had high self-esteem and liked having money to throw around," he says.

"I think watching the men dance gave them a feeling of superiority, of flipping the traditional roles and being in control in the gender game."

Just as female dancers know what they're looking for in a customer, so the men were always looking to hit the jackpot with one wealthy woman. Because the Olympic Gardens didn't have a VIP room for women customers in the mid- to late-90s, the men would take them in the back and give lap dances. Javier says $2500 was the biggest score he heard about in one night, but of course that was money earned inside the club. What happened later, back in the hotel rooms or in parked cars, was another story.

Javier also worked for a time as a disc jockey in a gay nightclub on Charleston called Flex. In the gay clubs the male dancers are called go-go boys. The entertainment might be a drag queen show one night, followed by go-go boys the next. "I would see the guys from Flex dancing for a gay crowd there, and even leaving with men customers after hours," he says, "and then the next night those same guys would be dancing for women at the Olympic Gardens."

> *"The best tippers were women with professional careers . . . and liked to throw money around."*
>
> —JAVIER

When I question Javier further about the incident with the Mississippi couple, he resists admitting that what he did constituted an act of prostitution.

"You were paid $100 by a man to have sex with his wife," I say. "What would you call it?"

"No, he paid me a tip at the club and then invited me to entertain his wife," he says. "He didn't pay me for the sex. He paid me for the dancing."

Although Javier says security was enforced at Olympic Gardens, there were several times he witnessed dancers getting oral sex from customers or going down on women. "There were 15 guys on a shift and you can't keep track of them every second, so stuff did happen," he says. "You have to understand that there were seemingly conservative women who got so inebriated or caught up in the excitement that they would just suddenly reach into a dancer's g-string and put him in their mouth. Of course, if a guy was caught in the act he was fired immediately."

It wasn't just women who were drawn to the male revues at the Olympic Gardens. "There were plenty of gay men who went and also a large following of bisexual couples," Javier says. "There are a good number of men who like to see their woman with another man because they have cut some kind of deal where anything goes in the relationship."

Kevin and Kelley are an attractive young couple, ostensibly very much in love, who dated for a year before getting married in a Las Vegas wedding chapel in the fall of 2002. Kevin is 25, but looks 19. He has brown hair, a slight build, and extremely boyish features. He has a perpetual twinkle in his eye as he talks, as though he's constantly on the verge of laughter. Kelley just turned 23, but gets carded whenever she orders a drink. She is a pretty blonde, tall, with beautiful legs, and a soft and straightforward manner in conversation. You get the feeling she couldn't lie to you even if she were paid.

Kevin grew up in Orange County and admits he was an introvert in school, a kid totally into computers, and he was behind the curve sexually. He didn't lose his virginity until he was 21.

Kelley played clarinet in the jazz band in her Oregon high school, was also on the shy side, but did well academically and was thought of as a "good kid, not a troublemaker." She saved her virginity until she was 20. Kevin and Kelley say they clicked immediately after meeting, and soon after decided to go steady. That's where the conventional part of their story comes to a screeching halt.

This couple didn't meet at a malt shop or through a hookup with friends, but by Kevin's responding to an online advertisement for a phone sex company. A student at USC at the time, Kelley was paying her tuition by working as an operator for the company, fielding calls and fueling fantasies off a separate phone line in her apartment. "I had sex with Kevin the first time I met him," she says. "I was having sex with a lot of guys at that time, but I clicked emotionally with him right away."

Kevin nods in agreement. "It started off far more sexual than a normal relationship," he says, "but then it became more normal. After a few months we were emotionally involved and we didn't have a desire to see other people sexually."

When I ask Kelley about the phone-sex job, she scrunches her face like a teenager told to eat spinach. "It wasn't a very good job," she says. "I made only about two thousand dollars a month, and it requires a lot of energy to talk to men at that level." She says the secret is to keep the caller on the phone for an extended conversation because the charge was a little over two dollars a minute, of which she kept about half.

"It's hard because the company gives out free minutes to start the call so a lot of them hang up when those minutes are up. The trick is getting to know a person as quickly as you can, learning what he wants."

And what do most men want from phone sex? I ask.

"They all want to know what you like sexually," she says. "And they want to know the craziest thing you've ever done. And then they want to hear you orgasm on the phone. That can get pretty tough when you're getting 15 to 20 calls a day."

As Kevin and Kelley's relationship progressed, it was clear that both were eager to push their sexuality even further. Once out of high school and safely away from home and family they felt totally liberated, and having met on an open field of expression they craved the attention and pure pleasure that sex gave them.

"After we'd dated a while and were clearly in love, I came up with the idea that I'd like to watch Kevin with another woman," Kelley says. "So that brought up the idea of being with other people. And then the thought came to us that we were young and good-looking and as long as we were willing to do it, why shouldn't we make some money with it. We had already decided we wanted a change from Southern California, and Las Vegas was a natural choice, not too far away but far enough and open enough that we could test out our ideas."

Their first venue for marketing their bodies was online chat rooms, explaining to other chatters what they were willing to do for money, and for how much. But that strategy went nowhere. They quickly discovered that most people in chat rooms don't have the discretionary income to spend on sex, which partly explains why they spend so much time online. Chatters can experience human interaction for little or no cost. But then Kevin and Kelley found online commercial websites where they could advertise their services, and that became their avenue to drawing business. Here was a barely-legal looking couple offering themselves on an open market, and accessible in about a minute online, to a universe of sex-hungry visitors to Las Vegas.

So how, exactly, do they offer themselves as a package? "The idea of advertising ourselves as a couple is very effective and inspires people's curiosity," Kelley says, "because it makes our ad stand out from the thousands of single women or men who advertise on the Internet. And we've found that the vast majority of our customers, who are single men, are primarily heterosexual but have a bisexual-curiosity. The man might have wondered about being with another guy, but he's never done it before, and he sees Kevin as being a non-threatening way to test the waters."

> *Their first venue for marketing their bodies was online chat rooms.*

She says the typical customer is a male in his 40s or 50s who will ask them to start off having sex as a couple before he joins in. The charge is $350 for an hour, with condoms mandatory.

I ask Kevin when he realized he was bisexual.

"I'm not really sure I am," he says, smiling as always, "but for all practical purposes I am. Let's just say I prefer women, but I'll do men for money."

"Had you engaged in homosexual activities before the two of you turned professional?" I ask.

"No," he says. "The first time I gave a man oral sex was the first time we were paid for it."

I tell him that's hard to believe.

He just shrugs and says nothing.

I then ask if the client had any idea that he was paying for sex from a man who'd never had gay sex before.

"I didn't tell him," he says. "But he seemed satisfied."

"It's about fifty-fifty on which one of us the men are more interested in," Kelley says. "Kevin or me."

In the year they've been in business, Kevin and Kelley have never entertained even one unaccompanied woman client, and have been hired "only a few times" by married couples. While Kelley says she is not bisexual, she will play with the woman for a while to get things started, "but I make it clear I don't want to spend the whole hour with her. Usually, with another couple, Kevin and I will start off together, and the other couple will do their thing, and then we'll swap."

> *"The firt time I gave a man oral sex was the first time we were paid for it."*
>
> —KEVIN

Kevin says he has never worked alone with a male client, only in tandem with Kelley. Not surprisingly, she gets many requests to work alone, and Kevin is perfectly all right with that.

"When she gets a job I will drive her to the hotel," he says. "I will not meet the client or go to the room with her. I will wait in the casino, and she will call my cell phone once she gets to the room and has checked it out. And I need to hear from her within a reasonable amount of time from when the appointment should end. I have never yet had to go up to the room because she waited too long to call. There have been times where I've been anxious about what was going on, but we have never had any real problems so far. I think it's unlikely that something bad will happen."

Something bad did happen just two months after Kevin and Kelley started selling themselves in Las Vegas. They got arrested and spent the night in jail. A man made an appointment over the phone to meet them at The Mirage, and he asked questions about money. They got too explicit with their answers. Just as the session began, the door opened and another undercover Metro officer read them their rights and they were off to jail. They were released the next morning without having to pay a fine, thanks to their attorney, but now they provide all the information about what they will and will not do on their website and they'll answer no specific questions about money or sexual details over the phone. On their site Kelley says, for instance, that she speaks "just a little Greek, but she may have problems with some big words." This means that she will engage in anal sex, but not with a well-endowed man. It's the kind of code-speak that is intended to answer questions for interested clients without drawing heat from the law.

They agree that their youthful appearance is a big reason they draw a lot of business, that and the fact they are the only Las Vegas couple advertising. "We've never even met another couple who does what we do," Kevin says "We've seen a few online ads, but they disappear as quickly as they pop up."

The best thing about their profession, they say, is the time it affords them together. Kelley still likes to play music and Kevin watches football and sports and just chills out. With their first year in business coming to a close, they had earned about $65,000. Kelley calls it "not bad money for less than 10 hours of work per week. And we expect to do much better this year. The momentum is really starting to pick up."

The idea of visiting swing clubs doesn't appeal to either of them. "We'd go if a client paid us to," Kevin says, "but we prefer to be more private. Also, we've heard that there's a lot of unsafe sex going on there. You have to watch your backside." He laughs at his little joke.

The only downside for Kelley is that she is concerned about getting a sexually transmitted disease. "We practice very safe sex," she says, "but you never know." She also says that with all the business they've had lately her own sex drive with Kevin is down slightly. "So I let him have sex with other women when he wants," she says. "I don't have to be there when it happens. I want him to be happy."

Their first year they had earned about $65,000.

My strong sense is that this young couple is very much in love. Their body language is affectionate and they continually glance at each other throughout the interview as reassurance that they are saying the right things. But there's a part of me that can't help but wonder what the future holds for this high-wire act. Ten years from now will they have saved money from this walk on the wild side and settle into a more conventional business and lifestyle together? They say they'd like to do this gig for just five more years, and then raise a family. It seems highly unlikely from my sense of logic, but then everything about these two "kids" defies expectation.

As I leave the interview I feel about 110 years old. This is a different generation entirely, it seems to me, than the one I was raised in. These youngsters were raised on *MTV*, *Girls Gone Wild*, *Reality TV*, and the Internet, where getting naked and having sex at an early age is as normal as pancakes for breakfast.

My last question to them is, "Do either of your parents have any idea what you're doing for a living?"

"God no," says Kelley, with a wide-eyed look. "They'd never believe it."

"Huh-uh," says Kevin, still smiling — always smiling.

The conclusion I reached, after months of poking and prodding around, is that there is a small and highly closeted male prostitute population in Las Vegas. These men are available to both men and women, particularly older women, who in many cases want no more from an escort than to provide attractive and pleasant company for an evening out on the town, to take them to dinner or a show. These men operate on an hourly rate and get their referrals from the same corps of workers who provide most of the information to Las Vegas tourists, namely limo and cab drivers, bartenders, valet parkers, and bellmen. As far as the male skin trade goes, Las Vegas doesn't hold a candle to its California brothers San Francisco and Los Angeles.

An undercover Metro vice cop told me, "These guys do their thing very quietly, don't cause us any real trouble, and don't want anyone knowing much about their business."

He was telling me something I already knew.

It's All About the Benjamins

"The girl ain't no faker. She know how to shake that moneymaker."

— STANDARD RAP LYRIC

It's dark and cramped inside the Crazy Horse Too, one of the gentlemen's clubs that now dot the back roads near the Las Vegas Strip — one of 30 and counting. The low-ceilinged building is filled with women, semi-naked or naked-down-to-a-g-string, expressing various levels of indifference on this routine Friday night in late July. The mercury soared to the hundred and teens during the day, and is just now cooling down to body temperature. The lighting inside is colored and smoky, but still manages to bounce beads of light off the silver halter-top covering one dancer's huge breasts. Her platinum wig makes her stand out among nearly 200 women who've shown up for work this night, which is precisely why she wears it. The trick is to get the sucker's eye. Make him want you more than the others so that you can become his private dancer for 10 or 15 minutes and leave him with a reel full of fantasies and three hundred fewer dollars in his billfold. As the girls like to say, "It's All About the Benjamins."

> ## "Bigger tits mean bigger tips."
>
> –A PLASTIC SURGEON

If the customer doesn't get gratification in the club, it's better than even money he'll dial up a skin flick at his hotel room later on and take matters into his own hands. A man simply has to have sex every day when he goes to Las Vegas. If it were only gambling that brought him here, then why not just go to an Indian casino or a riverboat near wherever he lives to scratch that itch? It's the promise of hot steamy sex that separates Las Vegas in 2004 from the other 47 states that have legalized gambling.

More than half the girls this night can fill a D-cup with plenty spilling over. Bigger tits mean bigger tips in this game, according to a plastic surgeon who moved to Las Vegas from Beverly Hills two years ago. "I got tired of doing eye lifts and neck jobs on aging, out-of-work actresses," he tells me, after a round of golf. "In Vegas I can do three or four augmentations in a day. The money is much better and the customers are less demanding. It's hard to please women who come to you at age 55 and say, 'Make me young and beautiful again.' When you're a 50-year-old career actress in Hollywood, you either have great acting ability and learn to swallow your pride and play some younger-and-prettier starlet's mother, or you're history. It's much easier for a plastic surgeon to give an exotic dancer bigger boobs. With the increase in tips, she can recover the cost of the surgery in less than a month."

I ask the doctor, a handsome man in his early 40s, whether he ever dates his patients. "I have, yeah," he says, "but no more. I'm getting married next year…and no, I didn't meet her in a strip club."

I then ask whether his fiancée is troubled by the fact that his waiting room is packed with exotic dancers every day.

"I'll get back to you later on that one," he says.

Many of the dancers in "the Horse" are huddled near the entrance. At this early hour, just after nine p.m., they nearly outnumber the customers. The girls chat among themselves as casually as though they were gathered in a school cafeteria line. Only a few bother to mingle among the clientele, but one girl, who has chosen the unlikely name of Chastity, is strictly business. Over the next fifteen minutes, I watch her approach three different customers to solicit a lap dance, but they all act like they have fishhooks in their pockets. When the fourth prospect, a portly man in his 30s wearing a Tommy Bahama shirt and shorts, accepts her offer, she spends nearly an hour with him. After she's performed several dances and left him glassy-eyed and devoid of reason, I approach her and ask if she'd mind telling me how much she earned from Mr. Bahama.

"I'll tell you for ten dollars," she says with a coquettish grin, true to the credo that time is money in the big city. I decide that's a reasonable exchange, about the price of the second cocktail I'm about to order.

"One twenty-five," she says. "I could have made five hundred if I'd gone back to his hotel room with him." She slips the two finskies I hand her into the strap of her leather brassiere. "But I'm not that kind of girl."

I ask her how she selected her stage name. "I wanted a name that suggested innocence," she says. "Isn't that the ultimate fantasy for guys? To sleep with a virgin?"

A guy in his 20s, ruggedly handsome, with a bold tattoo of an attacking serpent on his right forearm, has his face mashed against the stomach of a lithe brunette, naked but for a dental floss g-string. She is performing a full-contact lap dance over him, sort of a body-surf across his face. It's far more intimate than the Clark County Commission would tolerate, with its 2002 resolution that ineffectively endeavored to put restrictions on the contact between a dancer and her client. (The actual ordinance, which was voted on without opposition on November 19, 2002, allows dancers to touch customers' buttocks, and also allows strippers to grind their anus, genitals, and pubic area against a customer's leg. It does not say that a girl can

Chapter 11

allow a customer to put a full-slobber face-plant all over her breasts and stomach, which is clearly happening here.) What the customer can't see from his prone position is that the object of his affection, whose face is fully two feet above him, is having a conversation with her girlfriend standing behind his chair. It's also clear that she's scanning the back of the room to find her next prospect, someone she can entice into the VIP room and turn her night around. She takes a quick peek at her watch, as though there's somewhere else she ought to be.

As one stripper says when I ask her if the job becomes as boring as a desk job, "It's just another day at the orifice."

I give the line a polite smile. She acts surprised that I don't think it's funnier than that.

"My father was a dentist," I explain. "And he used to say the same thing after a day of looking into people's mouths."

She thinks about that a minute, then responds with a line that merits a rim shot. "One thing dentists have in common with my customers," she says. "Is that they both want to fill my cavities."

I laugh at that one, and she seems flattered. "You can put that in your book," she says.

"I will," I say. Marker down.

Before I leave, I ask the comedienne her name, so I can give her full credit.

"My name's Summer," she says.

"Your real name?" I inquire.

"No, my real name is Spring," she says. "And then I got hotter."

I like this girl. The last thing I expect to find in a nightclub writhing with naked sweaty bodies is a poor man's Rita Rudner. I wonder if she doesn't watch the stand-ups on the cable channels and jot down

It's All About the Benjamins

their good lines, material she can steal and use on her customers to enhance her likeability and their gratuities. I tell her the next time the Improv has an exotic dancer night, she's a shoo-in for first prize.

An undercover cop named Michael has told me a lot of things about Las Vegas strip joints.

"It's an elaborate con game going on in those clubs," he says. "The girl's goal is to make a certain amount of money every night. She might be a two hundred-dollar girl, she might be a five hundred-dollar girl. I've heard there's a small number that pull in a grand a night. It all depends on how hot she is, and how fast she can hustle you back to the VIP room so she can really do a number on you. She doesn't care if you're good looking or a fat slob with boils on your neck. She'll pretend you're the only man in the world for the 30 minutes or two hours that you're paying her to dance for you. And if you're giving her more than twenty dollars per dance, she'll probably hang with you all night long. Unless you negotiate for sex, and she's the kind of girl willing to leave the club and go the distance with you, which is very possible, her job is to make you feel like a big stud and the only guy in the world for her as long as the cash is rolling.

> *"My name's Summer . . . my real name is Spring, and then I got hotter."*
>
> —Summer

"Apparently there are a lot of lonely men in the world who buy into this," Michael says, "because there's just a huge amount of money in the topless scene in Vegas these days. It's totally crazy."

                                          Chapter 11

Bianca Paris, who has been dancing for three years and is employed at Jaguars, understands perfectly how to make the most of her evening shift. She wants to take home at least a thousand dollars for her eight hours of dancing, and the way to do that is not by what she calls "onezies," her term for single dances at twenty dollars apiece, but "in chunks."

She says the key to making great money is "to spot the money and jump on it right away." A petite blonde, just five-foot-three and 103 pounds, but "five-eleven in my heels," she says the most important keys are body language and eye contact. "I'm looking for someone who is very interested in me," she says. "When I'm onstage, I'm like a hunter, a predator. Some girls go up there and act like they're in la-la land, but I'm scanning that crowd constantly. I'm looking to find a guy who can't take his eyes off me, and I'll lock eyes with him. And in case he moves when I'm not watching, I pay attention to what he's wearing so I can find him when I get offstage. Obviously, if a guy tips me $100 when I'm up there, I'll beeline it over to him when my routine is over because he deserves special attention."

> *"The key to making great money is to spot the money and jump on it right away."*
>
> —BIANCA PARIS

Once at the customer's table, Bianca says the ice-breaking scenario will go something like this: "I'll climb very seductively onto his leg, not saying a word. Then I'll lean into his ear, and pause for a second. I can already feeling his blood pressure going up and his body tensing up. Then I'll whisper, 'Hi.' This usually gets a giggle or a smile. Next, I want to know where he's from. If he's local, he's not going to spend a lot of money. So I'll ask him where he flew in from. And if he says

Cleveland, I'll say. 'Perfect. I'll bet you don't have girls like this in Cleveland.' Then I'll grab his wrist and apply pressure, and say, 'I'm twisting your arm for a dance.' And he'll usually say something like 'You don't have to twist my arm.'

"It's just a cute way of having an exchange to break the ice," she says. "I'm very aggressive and I pour on the body language. I'm not going to give him a chance to turn me down because I know he doesn't want me to hop off him."

As the undercover cop Michael has said, Bianca's goal is to get that man up to the VIP room as quickly as possible.

"I let the man know I'm not that available, that I have another man waiting for me in another part of the room," Bianca says, "but that I couldn't resist coming over to him. Men want to believe that this is true. Their egos feed on this sort of attention. And if the man wants to go to the VIP room, I tell him we have to go *right now*. I create a sense of urgency. And then he'll pay the $500 for the first hour, either in cash or on his credit card, and up we go."

Do most men assume that they're going to get more than intimate lap dances up there? I ask her.

"They always ask what they're getting in the VIP room," Bianca says. "I tell them it's more private, and that they can be more at ease without so many people around. Which of course is totally true. But if you tell a man or even imply to him that he'll have sexual freedom, or sexual satisfaction once he's up there, you're going to have a miserable hour because the man is going to be disappointed and grabby and feel like he's getting ripped off."

Bianca swears that in her more than two years in Las Vegas, working at four different clubs, she has never witnessed an act of prostitution.

Chapter 11

"I'm back in those rooms all the time," she says. "And I swear I haven't seen it. I have heard it's happened, but I've never witnessed it."

Of course, what girls do when they leave the clubs, where they go and with whom, is something the club owners aren't concerned about. "I think the girls that do provide sex do so because they feel they have to," she says. "They are either girls with low self-esteem, or they are in a desperate situation. I see it more with girls from different cultures, from some of the Russian girls who come here, and the Vietnamese. Some girls can't get the high-caliber guy they want to pay them good money just for dancing, so they take it further."

Unlike the vast majority of dancers in Las Vegas, Bianca Paris (it's her real, legal name, as hard as that may be to believe) didn't start dancing in her early 20s. She was nearly 36 years old when she made the decision to sell three hair salons she owned in Susanville, California, and embark on a new life.

Bianca's younger sister had been diagnosed with a brain tumor and as she was undergoing chemotherapy and radiation treatments, Bianca found herself taking a hard look at her own circumstances. "I thought about if I'd been told I had a short time to live, would I have any regrets?" she says. "There I was working six days a week, 10 hours a day running the salons. And on days off I would attend hair seminars so I could be the best I could be in my profession. But I didn't have a social life. Basically I was a workaholic. I decided then that I wanted more out of life, both more money and more excitement."

She had dabbled in small-time show business, doing live remotes for a Reno radio station and co-hosting a movie show called "Zombo's House of Horror" on KOLO-TV in Reno. She wore sexy garments and fetish gear at the show and got a lot of compliments about how sexy and perky she was. The gig was a way for her to scratch a performing itch.

When a girlfriend in San Francisco got a job in a bikini bar, where the girls dance topless onstage but keep their tops on for table dances, Bianca was curious about it. Her first thought was that she could never do it, and that nude dancing was a scandalous profession. But on a late visit one evening, she was impressed with the glamour of the place and the beauty and sensuality of the girls. She agreed to try it for a few dances and ended up earning $400 for three hours. She also found that she loved the performing aspect of dancing, and she was a natural tease with the customers.

The gig was a way for her to scratch a performing itch.

The place was called Boys Toys, and through the summer of 2001 Bianca averaged an astounding $1600 a night in tips, more than she made in a week as a hairdresser with her three salons.

"Our stage manager was a flaming black man named Edward, and he made us feel like it was real show business," she says. "There was a lot of emphasis on makeup and style and theatricality. I couldn't believe how great a job it was, then 9/11 happened and everything stopped."

Bianca says that business almost totally dried up because no one would drive over the suspension bridges to get to San Francisco anymore. "But I knew I'd found my calling, and so it was just a matter of relocating," she says. "Everyone was saying that Las Vegas was the place to go for a dancer. And so within a week after the crisis of 9/11, I moved to Vegas."

Bianca had already had one breast augmentation before she got here, going from a small B-cup to a small C. And she'd dyed her hair from black to Barbie blonde. But once here, and with firm monetary goals, she had her breast size increased again. "I went up to a full C," she says. "And my income and self-esteem went up with it. I probably averaged about $200 more per night after that second boob job. Why fight it? Men just love blonde hair and big tits. It's a fact of life."

Karin, a Las Vegas madam profiled earlier in this book, worked on and off as a stripper for 15 years. She says that a girl won't stay in it for long unless she has a certain exhibitionist streak.

"I didn't think I could ever dance naked in front of a lot of people," she says. "I always thought I was too shy. But the first time I got up and stripped on stage

> *"I didn't think I could dance naked . . . but the first time . . . it was a total thrill."*
>
> —KARIN

in a club in Los Angeles, it was a total thrill. It made me feel like a celebrity. For a girl with insecurities, there's no better feeling than looking down into men's faces and seeing their desire."

Karin also says that it's hard for young women to leave the profession once they start making good money. "The dance club has a way of becoming your entire existence," she says. "You're keeping late hours, so you're not out in the real world much in the morning or middle of the day. And the bartenders and other dancers become your social life. It's very insulated. And where else is the typical dancer, who usually doesn't have a lot of education or any clearly defined career goals, going to make the kind of money she'll make in a club? Most of the girls don't save their money the way they should, and so they get trapped in a lifestyle that demands that they keep dancing for that three hundred or five hundred a night."

Lexy and Brenda, who work for Karin as top-dollar call girls, both tell me that dancing is beneath them. Brenda tried it for two nights at Cheetah's and says, "I absolutely hated it. I resented the fact that men could stand there all night and stare at me naked without paying a cent. I thought the whole scene was totally sleazy."

Lexy says, "I would never dance topless. Yuk. It's hard work, the hours are long and you're expected to be there all the time, and the money isn't that good. I can make in an hour or two what those girls make in a week."

I paraphrase Brenda and Lexy's comments about stripping to Sabrina Markey, who is probably the most visible and best-known stripper in Las Vegas. She laughs out loud.

"Isn't that funny?" she says. "Here these girls are hooking, and they're looking down at my profession, which I consider an art form. But hey, it's cool. I'm all for sexual freedom in whatever form it takes as long as there are no victims."

Sabrina is stunning, the kind of woman a nightclub owner considers "the full package." She's five-foot-nine, with a voluptuous, athletic body, and alluring, ethnically blended features. Her father is Hawaiian-Japanese, and her mother a full-blooded Norwegian, and as so often happens their offspring took on the best features of each. She has the smooth light brown skin and almond eyes of a

Chapter 11

Polynesian princess, and the long toned legs of a cross-country skier. And thrown into the mix is a type-A personality that drives her to get the most out of anything she tries.

Sabrina describes herself as "a girl who followed all the rules." She went to a private prep school in Hawaii and graduated from the University of Southern California in the early 1990s with a degree in international business and a minor in Japanese. Her first job was with a company in New York that paid her a starter's salary and promised her quick advancement if she performed.

Perform she did, but not in the way her bosses anticipated. She had been in Manhattan just three weeks when some friends suggested they all go to a famous gentlemen's club called Scores. (Radio junkies may recognize the place as Howard Stern's favorite hangout.)

As fate would have it, on her very first visit to a strip joint, a club patron begged the manager to get Sabrina onstage for one quick dance. He was offering $500 to watch her take it off.

"Seeing as I was making just barely more than that in one week at my job, I was intrigued by the offer," she tells me, as we chat over a latte' at a Starbucks on the west side of Las Vegas. "I took a few shots of tequila for fortification, and up I went. I was shaking like a leaf, but the customers were going crazy. The man actually kept getting stacks of dollar-bills from the bar and before I had finished he had thrown three thousand one-dollar bills onto the stage. It looked like all the money in the world."

Sabrina realized that very night that dancing was going to provide a far quicker route to the financial goals she had set for herself upon graduation. She called in sick at her job every day for the next week and danced every night.

She then took "a permanent leave of absence," from the company that had lured her to New York, and worked full-time at Scores. Three weeks later she accepted an offer to dance at the first strip club in downtown Tokyo, called Club Orange. It was a private, members-only club, and American girls like Sabrina were at a premium. She had her own personal driver and complimentary hotel room, and unlike most gentlemen's clubs, Club Orange even paid her a salary. (In Las Vegas, dancers pay the club owner a daily "house fee," ranging from $25 up to $60 at Jaguars, where Sabrina is currently employed.)

Over the next couple of years, she danced all over the world — in Mykonos, Greece; in London; at different locations in Japan; in Miami and Atlanta and Dallas. Strip clubs were becoming more and more popular, taking on the less offensive label of "gentlemen's clubs." Fortune 500 executives thought nothing of taking clients there on a regular basis for business lunches. They were discovering that two martinis and a lap dance could go a long way toward securing a client's loyalty. It's the oldest form of male bonding there is, ogling gorgeous women and talking about what you could do with them alone and naked, and in the cusomer's fantasy, they are both.

> *It's the oldest form of male bonding there is, ogling gorgeous women.*

And more and more young women, like Sabrina — girls who never would have considered taking off their clothes in public a generation before — were able to rationalize working weekends or summer vacations for a thousand dollars a night. They could use the money to put themselves through school, or to better provide for those two little ones who arrived so soon after their mom married her high-

Chapter 11

school sweetheart, but before she realized that marriage wasn't all it was cracked up to be.

Sabrina estimates that at least a couple hundred coeds from her alma mater USC, and from UCLA, fly to Las Vegas on weekends or during busy conventions to dance. "And why shouldn't they?" she says. "It beats working in the student union." Although some consider the Forum Shops at Caesars Palace to be the best people-watching venue in Las Vegas, single men might consider the Southwest Airlines gate at McCarran International Airport on Friday afternoons and Sunday evenings. That's when the coeds from Southern Cal and Arizona State, and some of the Texas colleges, fly into town with their little overnight bags and makeup kits.

"You can spot them in a minute," an airline gate attendant told me. "They all have cute faces and perfect hair and nice upright titties, and they look more like pageant girls than strippers. If these clubs were ever shut down for any reason, Southwest Airlines' stock would nose-dive."

⁓⥢⌇⌁

Sabrina decided to move to Las Vegas in 1996 because she felt it was the only place in the world where she could make the kind of money she made in Tokyo, when she was starting out.

"If you're going to be a dancer, there's no better place in the world to be than Las Vegas," she says. "The men who come into the clubs are mostly gamblers, and they compare the time they spend with you to their time at the tables. They might be playing five thousand dollars a hand or more. And if a man gives you a couple thousand dollars for a few hours of pleasure and diversion, it's just like he lost one hand of blackjack. The criteria here are just so different than any place else. And no matter what the economy is like in the rest of the country or world, Vegas is a place where people have no qualms about spending money.

"I had a guy one night who tipped me fifteen thousand dollars for one hour in the VIP room," she says. "And he got nothing more than a bunch of slow lap dances. That's just an obscene amount of money, I know, but it actually happened."

Was he a regular customer? I ask.

"Nope. Just a guy from New York in his 40s who was a big gambler," she says. "I wish he was a regular. I'd sure love to see him again."

> *Sabrina tipped the bouncers $3,000 that night.*

Sabrina tipped the bouncers three thousand dollars that night. "It's something you need to do," she says. "Tipping in this city is what makes it all work. You can't get greedy. It will come back to you."

Jaguars is Sabrina's fifth dance gig in Las Vegas. She's also been employed at The Playpen, Crazy Horse Too, Olympic Gardens, and Club Paradise. She's happy at Jaguars, she says, "Because (a) the security is good. They even have a minimum height and weight requirement for security guards, and (b) Our VIP room is the most expensive in town. I make $500 an hour minimum when I get a customer to go in there."

And what type of customer is she looking for?

"My general clientele is between ages 35 and 50," she says. "It's the guy who comes into the club alone or with one other friend, never part of a large group. And he is not wearing a suit. I'm especially suspicious of a man wearing a suit in this town between May and September, because he's got to be burning up. Obviously, he's trying too hard to impress. My ideal customer is just nicely dressed and almost always from out of town. I try to avoid the locals because they bring issues with them. First you become their favorite dancer for a night, then their special friend, then they start to fall in love with you. Next thing you know they've broken up with their girlfriend and want you to marry them. And if you're not careful, you end up with a stalker. And that's a big problem in our profession.

"I've only been burned once in Las Vegas," she says. "And that's when a girl I thought was my friend gave my address to a customer for a thousand dollars. But I learned from that, and I'm more careful now. I'm not in this business to make friends, but to make money."

In July 2002, Sabrina decided to open a business she calls Stripper 101. It's a group of classes that teach a wide range of women how to take off their clothes, either for money or for fun. She has a class

> "I try to avoid the locals because they bring issues with them."
>
> — SABRINA

for aspiring professional dancers that includes information about auditioning, table dancing, lap dancing, pole work, stage presentation, working a VIP room, learning how to maintain and interact with clients, and how to budget money and plan retirement.

She also offers sessions for currently employed dancers who want to become feature dancers, which includes lessons in planning and choreographing a show, choosing the right costumes (and logging what costumes were worn for the best customers, so that it can be determined how effective they were), and even finding the right booking agent for international travel.

And she offers a "housewife special," for the woman who wants to put a little spice in her marriage or just wants to learn how to move better or get in better shape. Students discover how they can change their look through cosmetics. They learn how to plan for that big night, and set up a room in the home for a stage. Most important, they learn seductive lap dance techniques. Sabrina recently enrolled a 72-year-old woman in her housewife special, and says, "She absolutely rocked. She was awesome."

> *Sabrina recently enrolled a 72-year-old woman. "She absolutely rocked. She was awesome."*
>
> — SABRINA

The price for the professional dancers is $300 for nine hours of instruction over three days, and the "amateurs" pay $200 for six hours over two days.

All heights, weights, and shapes are welcome to enroll in Strippers 101. "Men like all types and nationalities of women," she says, "so I'll never discourage someone based on their size or appearance. But I do believe a girl has to have a commanding presence and be able to speak intelligently. Verbal communication and meeting people in a nice way is a huge part of making money in the clubs. I know there are girls who make money off the dumb blonde routine, and I can throw my hair and talk in a breathy voice with the best of them if I have to, but please don't make me play the stupid stripper act. I find it demeaning."

She says her inspiration to teach the class came from an older stripper in New York, who pulled her aside when she first started dancing and told her, "Don't be stupid in this business, or it will eat you alive. One day it will end and you have to be ready."

The woman gave Sabrina the name of her broker, her accountant and her lawyer, and right from the beginning, rather than giving her money to a boyfriend or spending it frivolously, she has been building a portfolio of mutual funds, CDs, and what she calls "really conservative investments." She also likes to invest in real estate and owns homes in Las Vegas, Southern California, and Hawaii, which is where she intends to move in two or three years when her other businesses, such as a cosmetics company for strippers called Eye Candy, and an internet business she's just launching, exceed her earnings from dancing.

"It's tricky," she says, "because I would have thought I'd be out of it by now. But I have so many good regular customers that are loyal to me that it's tough to just turn off that income stream. Realistically, I'd say I'll dance for another two or three years, at most."

She estimates that the average annual income for a dancer in Las Vegas who works four nights a week, year round, is $85,000, and that the top girls make over $250,000. It becomes obvious after five minutes with Sabrina why she's at the top of the pay scale.

Sabrina says that a common misconception housewives harbor about her classes is that they think that topless dancing is a totally integrated part of the sex industry, and that as a professional she has the answers to every sex problem imaginable. "I have women that come in and ask me where they can buy dildos, and will I show them how to use them," she says, laughing. "I tell them, 'Honey, that's not the business I'm in. I can give you suggestions, but I'm not going to teach you how to play with yourself.'"

It's All About the Benjamins

Sabrina and Bianca Paris tell me something else that I was surprised to hear. They both say that "about ninety percent" of the female exotic dancers in Las Vegas are bisexual. "That's part of the draw of the business," another unnamed stripper tells me. "Bisexual women like to be around other women with their clothes off. And we love it when women come into the club. They make up a good share of our income."

Bianca goes so far as to say "about a third of my lap dances are done for women, and I really enjoy doing them." Although she claims she is not bisexual, she says, "Women customers make me laugh. I'm very comfortable with them, and they tend to be more handsy than men. Usually, they're with their guy when I'm dancing for them, and it's a form of foreplay that they go through to enhance their own lovemaking when they go back to the hotel. There's just no bigger turn on for a guy than to see his woman with another hot woman. The only time I don't like it is when the woman isn't wearing panties, and that's too often the case because the guy she's with likes her that way."

The reason Bianca thinks she has so many women customers is because of her small size and the fact that she puts forth positive energy. "Women and their men like the Barbie doll look," she says. "But if the woman is real big she'll never choose me for a dance because I just emphasize her bigness. I've only been dancing for less than three years, but I feel like I understand exactly how this business works."

It's an August night, about ten-thirty, hotter than Hades, and I stop three men coming out of Olympic Gardens on the north end of the Strip. I explain that I'm writing a book and would like to ask them a few questions. They are about to get into a cab, so I slip the driver a tip for detaining his fare. He says, "It's cool, Bro. I ain't leavin' till they are."

The men are from Conway, Arkansas, and they are in town for a buddy's bachelor party that is being held two days hence.

The youngest of the three, a fellow about 25 wearing a golf visor, asks me if all the strippers in town are as fine as the ones inside the OG.

"There are a lot of beautiful dancers in this town," I say.

"I'd have proposed to about six of the girls in there," he says. He then shoves his right hand into his pocket and adjusts himself. "Shit, I've had a diamond-cutter since I first walked in the place. Do you know where we can get laid?"

I dodge the question and inquire how much they've spent in the two hours they were in the club. When they total it up, using rough estimates of course, they figure that between the three of them, on booze and lap dances combined, they've spent about seven hundred dollars.

> *"But you're not thinkin' about the money … I guess that's a lot to spend to get a case of blue balls."*
>
> –Visiting Cowboy

"Was it worth it?" I ask

"Yeah, we had a blast," says one of them, a slender fellow wearing a cowboy hat who introduces himself as Cody. "But you're not thinkin' about the money when you have a stone fox stuffing her 44 double Denvers right in your face. I guess that's a lot to spend to get a case of blue balls."

His buddies laugh heartily at this assessment.

After a few more minutes of idle chitchat, the men ask the cabbie how much it will cost to drive them to Pahrump, where there are legal houses of prostitution. I overhear him suggest that there's a swingers' club nearby that will save them the trouble and serve the same purpose. By the time the sun comes up, these jovial boys from Razorback Country will have poured about two thousand dollars into the Las Vegas economy.

Sabrina Markey has heard a lot about the effort to unionize strippers in Las Vegas. The movement is headed by a 50-year-old dancer named Andrea Hackett, who is the founder and executive director of the Las Vegas Dancer's Alliance. Because of her cause and the unusual circumstances of her life, Hackett has drawn considerable attention from the national media. She has been interviewed by CBS News, the *L.A. Times*, the *Washington Post*, and *Nation* magazine.

> *"I know I'm the only nude dancer in Vegas who went to Woodstock and who burned her draft card."*
>
> –ANDREA HACKETT

Hackett makes good copy not only because her cause is tantalizing, but because she used to be a man. She underwent a sex change operation in 1995, and in 2003 told *The Nation* magazine, "I know I'm the only nude dancer in Vegas who went to Woodstock and who burned her draft card."

Hackett was outraged that the Clark County Commission voted to regulate stripping and lap dancing, an industry that brings millions of dollars monthly into the area's coffers. She has the full support of the ACLU in her fight for freedom of expression, and from AFL-CIO officials who have shown interest in having the dancers join their ranks. She also published a "Dancers Voter Guide" for the November '02 election and registered nearly 500 dancers to vote.

The strong suspicion of the pro-dancers movement is that the commission action was instigated by power brokers along the Strip, who can't be overjoyed that the gamblers for whom they provide complimentary room, food, and beverage, are spending increasingly larger parts of their Vegas vacations and discretionary income, not in their host casinos, but in gentlemen's clubs.

Sabrina agrees with Hackett on the impact of Las Vegas strippers on the local economy. "Following September 11, dancers poured a ton of money into retail stores when a lot of other people were staying home," she says. "I haven't met a stripper yet who didn't know how to shop till she dropped."

But Markey is totally against unionizing strippers. "I'm self-reliant," she says. "I don't need or want a union's involvement in my career. I determine by my effort and by tending to my business just how much I'm going to make in this profession. I think the union idea is supported by girls who want to be pulled up to a higher level, and by those who aren't running their business right. Maybe they're too old, or not in shape, or have bad attitudes." She pauses for a minute, and then says, "Or maybe they need to take my class to learn how to run their business properly. I just don't believe unions are the answer."

She agrees with the assessments of other power brokers that the day is near when classy gentlemen's clubs will be contained within the Strip hotels. "I think either George Maloof or Steve Wynn will find a way to do it," she says. "And when they do I'm the perfect person to hire the girls and manage the club. I've been training for a position like that my whole career."

It's All About the Benjamins

She finds it sad that only about ten percent of the dancers she knows really understand how to manage their money, or invest for the future. "And it used to be lower than that," she says. "The girls are really getting better now that there are so many of them and they can discuss issues among themselves."

In the enrollment packet for her Strippers 101 classes Sabrina devotes an entire section of the curriculum to Money: Her advice begins thusly: "The point of working in this business is NOT to make friends, feel better about yourself, or to get in a good work-out. The ONLY reason you should ever do this job is TO MAKE MONEY!!!![*sic*] There is a lot of real money to be made and even on your WORST night, you'll still be making more money than you ever did cocktailing, sitting at a computer, or whatever your job is now."

Markey also provides handout forms on which the dancer can keep daily and monthly reports on data such as earnings, amount tipped out, and the names of new customers. Sabrina keeps a huge file of business cards and each year sends Christmas cards to more than 500 clients.

"The key to sustaining a good income as a dancer month in and month out, and staying somewhat recession-proof, is keeping regular customers," she says. "They make up the biggest part of my business."

She says it's a sad fact that about fifty percent of the dancers she knows support lazy husbands or boyfriends. "So many of these men just sit at home and do nothing," she says. "It's hard for me to understand because eventually the girl loses respect for the man and he loses respect for himself. I always encourage these girls to either kick the guy out or make him get a job. But it rarely happens."

 Chapter 11

Bianca Paris admits that she was frivolous with her money the first year she was dancing. "When you go from making about fifty grand a year, as I did in the hair salon business, to over two hundred thousand a year, you have to be careful you don't spend it all on luxury items and frivolous things. I bought everything my little heart desired that first year," she says. "but I don't anymore."

Bianca says she now has a budget of four thousand a month, for her car, apartment, and necessities, and that she saves approximately 16 thousand dollars a month, which she is putting into commercial real estate.

"The reason I agreed to talk to you is because I wanted you to realize there is some discipline in this industry," she says. "The girls who are screw-ups weed themselves out pretty fast. But I've found that seventy percent of the dancers are fun-loving, happy people, not mentally ill, but fairly well centered, and by and large they are more carefree and stress-free than people in the regular business world. People think strippers catfight all the time. That's not true. We laugh a lot, because we're all making great money!"

Several of the women interviewed for this book either make their entire income or a good portion of it from dancing in gentlemen's clubs. As in every other level of what we'll loosely call show business, there is a star system on the gentlemen's club circuit that pays big money to name performers.

About 15,000 women dance part-time or full-time in the Las Vegas clubs, and most make the better part of their income from table dancing, or lap dancing. But some Las Vegas residents, like

Ashlyn Gere, Angela Summers, Christi Lake, and Anna Malle, all of whom we met earlier in the book, work as featured performers on the road. They get marquee billing and their pictures appear in newspaper ads days and weeks before their arrival to trumpet their appearances. Usually, these women perform three or four 20-minute shows per night as the headliner, and are contracted a set fee per show, anywhere from $150 all the way up to $500 or $1,000. In addition, they earn significant income from the sale of autographed pictures, autographed videos, even signature toys and panties. Men will pay more if they are assured the panties have been worn by the star. One stripper told me she buys a spray called "Scent of a Woman" which she uses on the panties and when the customer takes a whiff, it instantly doubles the price she can charge.

About 15,000 women dance part-time or full-time in the Las Vegas clubs.

Christi Lake peddles her signature vibrator after her dance appearances. The gizmo has 10 speeds and is guaranteed to please. (There's something oddly amusing to think of a man bringing home a special vibrator that he purchased at a strip club for his wife or girlfriend, but Christi says they sell like hotcakes.)

Some 20 years ago, the way a girl achieved featured-dancer status was by becoming a centerfold in one of the more explicit men's magazines like *Penthouse* or *Hustler*. But that all changed in the '80s with the introduction of home video machines. Once men and couples were allowed to rent adult videos and watch them in the privacy of their homes, the centerfolds were replaced by porn actresses on the dance circuit.

Chapter 11

Video rentals accessible at your corner video mart also killed the adult theaters that showed XXX rated movies for the so-called "raincoat crowd." Las Vegas had two such theaters in the downtown area.

As a sign of how times have changed, it is worth recalling that an early 1980s XXX star named Annette Haven made a personal appearance at one of these downtown Vegas theaters. I had appeared with her on a local talk show that afternoon, and found her a bright and lively conversationalist. When she invited me to catch her show that night, I accepted. (She happened to share with me that she was being paid just $300 plus expenses for the appearance.)

The evening began with a double-bill of adult films starring Haven, both running about 50 minutes in length. She then appeared onstage and did a gradual strip tease that lasted about 10 minutes, or three songs. It was a tasteful performance, more along the lines of a Gypsy Rose Lee dance than a modern-day

> *Video rentals killed the adult theaters that showed XXX rated movies.*

graphic display of internal organs. She then took questions from the audience. I would estimate there were 75 men in the theater, and no women. And I'd be lying if I didn't report there was some autoeroticism going on in the theater during the movies. It was exactly the type of theater in which the child star Pee Wee Herman was busted years later. I would imagine the janitors were equipped with mops as well as brooms, if you catch my drift.

Some 20 years later, a Las Vegas-based dancer named Lynn Chase, whose stage name is Venus De Light, told me in an interview that "You have to be a porn star to make the big money in dancing today." She says it started when a club owner a few years ago booked a popular adult star named Amber Lynn as a headliner. "She was a strong performer with a large following of adult film fans and she made terrific money, as much as $20,000 a week," Chase says.

Chase, who was inducted into the Stripper's Hall of Fame at the annual Gentleman's Club Exotic Dancer Awards show and is considered something of a legend in her profession, says at one time she was the highest paid dancer who was not a porn star. She made about $500 per day at the peak of her career.

"The performer who changed the whole nature of the industry, and the pay structure, was Marilyn Chambers," says Tony Indovino, owner of the Lee Network, the company that represents adult film stars on the dance circuit. "Marilyn absolutely tore it up and packed every house she played in," he says, "and that opened everyone's eyes in the business."

Indovino recalls a night when Chambers was performing at a club in Toronto, and the club was packed with 600 people, at an admission price of $25 a head. "Outside, there were another 200 people in knee-deep snow waiting to get in," he says. "This went on for four or five days, and I think it was that particular show that let promoters know there was a huge audience of adult film fans who couldn't wait to see the stars in person. (It's worth noting that Chambers parlayed her porn-star celebrity into legitimate dinner-theater appearances at the Union Plaza in downtown Las Vegas.)

Today, Indovino's company represents about 120 dancers, some 90 percent of them adult film stars. Among his clients are porn legends Amber Lynn and Ginger Lynn, who recently was the subject of a two-hour documentary on the E! television network. Indovino also books Jenna Jameson, a Las Vegas native who started stripping at the Crazy Horse Too in Las Vegas at just 17 years old, and has risen to become the undisputed number one star in the adult film world.

Jameson, who also was the subject of a two-hour E! documentary that first aired in August 2003, has become a multimillionaire from her heated performances in dozens of films, many pictorials in graphic men's magazines, and her own website, called Club Jenna, which serves as an international checkout desk for her many videos and other sexually related items. The first film that Jenna's new production company produced, called *Brianna Loves Jenna*, quickly sold over 100,000 DVDs, an unheard of figure for a XXX product.

Indovino says that Jameson has made as much as $4,000 per show on the dance circuit. Compare that with Annette Haven's meager $300 per night fee of 25 years ago, and it says something about the popularity of the genre. When you calculate Jameson's fee over a weekend, which would include three performances a night on a Thursday-through-Saturday gig, she's earning $36,000, not counting the sales of videos, Polaroid pictures taken on a customer's lap, and other sexual toys and paraphernalia that carries the star's brand or image. The cover charge for Jenna Jameson's show can go as high as $40, but as one pornophile told me, "Jenna's the Michael Jordan of the business. She's the hottest woman on the planet."

Christi Lake, who has made 300 adult films and danced on the national circuit for five years, confirms that the range of pay for most film stars onstage goes from $200 per show to over $1,000. Lake says that even seven years ago, when she started dancing, there were a limited number of film stars booked on the dance circuit. "But now the industry is inundated with so many new girls cranking out films that it's hard to keep track of them all."

How long can a porn star dance for the big bucks? "As long as her body holds up and her fans want to see her," Indovino says. "Amber Lynn, for one, has reinvented herself. She ran into some rough road about five years ago, but she got sober and reinvented herself."

Tony says that with the popularity of the Internet and adult websites, these veteran stars are receiving a whole new round of publicity. "All these new porn aficionados can discover a semi-retired actress and start buying her tapes off the Internet. And then when she comes through town for a dance engagement, they want to see her in the flesh."

> *It would appear that for the club girls dancing in Las Vegas, a saturation point . . . might not be too far off.*

It would appear that for the club girls dancing in Las Vegas, a saturation point where supply outweighs demand might not be too far off.

"I don't see it ever coming back to the level of income it was at before 9/11," says Bianca Paris. "Stripping has become so mainstream in Las Vegas that when I tell someone what I do it's no different than telling them I'm a bank teller. No one is ever surprised. I mean, the biggest star in Hollywood in the '90s, Demi Moore, played a stripper in a movie, and Christina Aguilera's last concert tour was called "Stripped and Justified." It's not a shocking thing anymore. And men who come to the clubs are not that enamored. It used to be they'd look at you and their jaw would drop. Now, they've seen so much skin you really have to work hard to engage them in conversation.

"But don't misunderstand," she says. "I'm going to dance as long as I possibly can. Where else can I make this kind of money and feel like a star?"

Clearing My Conscience

It's one of the indelible attractions for those of us who call Las Vegas home, the fact that we don't have to go anywhere else, that sooner or later the world will arrive at our doorstep.

There's a gossip columnist in town, a fellow named Norm who sports a black eye patch, who will inform readers of the *Las Vegas Review Journal* that every single night of the week, while Las Vegans are tucked safely in their beds, or working the graveyard shift at the titanium plant, or collecting keno tickets at the Golden Goose, people like Britney Spears and George Clooney and Beyonce Knowles and Ashton Kutcher and Jennifer Lopez are shaking their perfectly rounded uber-booties in an exotic nightclub somewhere on or near the Strip, doing everything in their limited power to keep alive the reputation that Vegas is Party Central, and that locals are just an orgasmic yodel away from a hotel room where beautiful people are having wild sex with other beautiful people. If vicarious thrills are for you, Las Vegas will provide round the clock goose bumps. And there's no safer sex than that being enjoyed by others.

It's no coincidence that both NBC's *Dateline* and ABC's *Prime Time Live* chose to focus their Fall 2003 premieres on Las Vegas, with a strong emphasis on the Sin City aspect. It's precisely what the viewing public wants to see, and no civic-minded citizen should object, as it generates great business for the Strip. Last August when *Prime Time's* producers heard there was a long-time local resident writing a book called *Skin City*, they kept me on the phone for two full hours, mining my research about how we came to be "the naughtiest place in America" in the year 2003. I explained to them repeatedly that while there were certainly sins of the flesh occurring in Las Vegas at the rate of 10,000 an hour 'round the clock, there are also more than a million residents who lead completely normal, traditional lives, waking each morning not in the company of hookers or dominatrixes or nameless strangers they'd played organ hockey with the previous night, but with family members whose value systems wouldn't differ one iota from those found in Boise or Kansas City. But stories about conventional behavior don't make good TV, or lofty ratings, so that stuff gets muted. (A random observation: I know it's called "reality TV," but how real are the lives of Anna Nicole Smith and Ozzie Osbourne? If those folks represent the real world, book me on the next shuttle to Neptune.)

Instead, *Dateline* chose to put a hidden camera on a man named Richie, who likes to call himself Cheese Whiz (I would assume he chose the moniker because it makes him feel hip-hop and happening, rather than his uncool reality of being a bespectacled pudgy white boy, whose only hope of ever getting laid is to fork over a wad of cash.) Cheese Whiz admitted to *Dateline* reporter Keith Morrison that he had spent $150,000 hiring prostitutes over the last year, but then decided to kick the habit when one of his favorite call girls, who went by the name of Alexis, was found murdered. Her untimely demise had made Cheese Whiz feel that perhaps being a full-time John was not the best thing to be. Hey, at least *Dateline* provided the guy his 15 minutes of fame, albeit as a conspirator against the very girls he'd been patronizing.

While *Prime Time* did balance its story by doing interviews with a Mormon bishop and a mother who expressed concern about a Jaguars rolling billboard, featuring a large-breasted stripper — parked right across from her church, for godsake — the emphasis of the piece was on the hundreds of millions of dollars being earned by the topless clubs, and how the LVCVA was promoting licentious behavior with the ad campaigns.

The sum effect of both shows was that you could almost hear keyboards clicking throughout the country as single men and couples looking for adventure logged on the Internet to book their next flights to Las Vegas. Just keep spelling the name right, folks, and never forget that television packages on Las Vegas assure lofty ratings during a sweeps period.

The closest I came to living in the belly of the beast of the stereotypical Las Vegas was the summer I dealt blackjack on the graveyard shift at the Four Queens Hotel and Casino. Although the nation was celebrating its Bicentennial, I was in the throes of a mid-20s identity crisis, trying to make sense of the circumstances that had ushered me from a respectable newspaper job in the Pacific Northwest to the bowels of Glitter Gulch, where I found myself issuing playing cards to dyspeptic customers for a dollar a hand. I wore a mask of misery as I stood behind that blackjack table, arms crossed, at 4 a.m. The intent was to scare off dealer-shoppers, those innocent amateur gamblers looking for a friendly face, someone who would at least make pleasant conversation while taking their money. My uniform was the standard issue orange necktie and green apron. At six-foot three, I looked like a giant carrot in a Veggie Tales movie.

On my 15-minute breaks that summer I would loiter outside the hotel, by the front entrance near the Big Six wheel, and watch the people go by; the tourists with their coupon booklets and plastic cups full of quarters; the occasional "working girl," as joyless and hardened by it all as I was becoming; and the drifters who shuffled along the pavement with their heads down, as much to spot stray

Afterword

coins as to bemoan their lot in life. All of the faces were distinct, even at 3 in the morning, bathed in the fluorescent light from the 45 miles of neon that wrapped itself around downtown. I imagined I could see right through the passersby, and they through me. Every so often I'd feel one of them staring back, wondering what this lanky guy in the dealer's apron was doing with his life as he stood there sipping his Dr. Pepper. Up to no good, they seemed to be thinking...or maybe that's what I was thinking about myself.

That summer I was a stranger to darkness. As I'd drive home at 6 in the morning, the sun would just be breaking over Sunrise Mountain; and as I'd drive to work at 8:30 the same night — although, of course, it seemed like the next day — there was but a sliver of natural light left in the sky. Turning off the expressway onto Main Street, I would enter the most intensely lit block of real estate on earth. I was reminded of a line from Goethe: "Where there is a great deal of light, the shadows are deeper." Unlike many, I had no desire to curse the darkness. I just wanted to embrace it and return it to its proper place in my life — at the end of the day.

I lasted just five months as a low-rent croupier. In the fall of that year I was hired to teach writing and literature at UNLV — for even less money than I'd made in the pit — and I started sending freelance articles to national magazines. When I got my first acceptance, from a literary journal in New York, I had to smile at the sweet irony of it all. The essay was titled "The Art of Dealing Blackjack." Little did the editors know that the artisan was one of the most misanthropic and least accommodating 21 dealers in gambling history.

Even back then, I knew that some day I wanted to explore the darker side of Las Vegas, but little did I know that it would be more than a quarter century before I would be able to screw up the courage to delve into the lives of those who tread on that dark side. There would be 11 years of editing a city magazine that, like the current publication *Las Vegas Life*, did everything in its power to portray Las Vegas as a well rounded, albeit culturally deprived, city coming of age.

And that would be followed by years of writing articles for national magazines about the changing face and bustling economy of the city that was gradually becoming known for more than just its casinos and two shows a night. Perhaps it was a stern Catholic upbringing that kept me until now from looking deeper into the bowels of Las Vegas. The matters we've discussed in this book would have been considered completely taboo where I was from. There's still a part of me that feels I should confess my sins to a priest for even having *thought* about writing this book. But the itch was always there, and it feels good to have finally scratched it.

While we always talk about two Las Vegases — and indeed there may be no city that can change its face more quickly to suit the occasion — I had subconsciously avoided the seedy side, but once I opened the box I quickly learned what Pandora had warned about.

While there has always existed a graveyard shift in Las Vegas, never was it considered the playground that it is today. Workers in past decades who signed off at anywhere from three a.m. to seven typically went home and crawled into bed until early afternoon, when they would rise and take care of their daily chores until punching in for work after the normal dinner hour. But today, with the rise of all the after-hours joints and chi-chi nightclubs in the hotels, a true party

Afterword

animal, whether Las Vegas resident or tourist bent on wringing 24 hours of pleasure out of his or her visit, has unlimited options.

"We've always had topless bars in Las Vegas, but they were off the beaten track and weren't an option for the masses," says Steve Wynn, as he looks out over the construction of his latest megaresort, Wynn Las Vegas, slated to open in spring oh-five. "But then places like the Crazy Horse Too started getting popular, and they provided the element of contact and personal involvement. A guy could sit next to a beautiful girl and even touch her. That's what the old nudie clubs didn't have. And that interactivity aspect of it, the close and intimate contact, is what has caused all these limousines to be parked at the clubs."

Wynn says the Strip hotels initially reacted by developing nightclubs and discos and lounges that also promised contact, albeit on a slightly more discreet basis. The scantily clad hostesses in these ultra-bars sit at the table as they take orders, or even kneel in front of the customer, implying a form of submission that can bolster a sagging male ego.

"In the '70s and '80s there was no real graveyard shift in town," Wynn says. "If you spent any money at those hours you'd just be wasting it. And this new craze is not about prostitutes, either. We've had them forever in Las Vegas. During the 80s and 90s when those sleazy guys were distributing escort-service pamphlets up and down they Strip, they never made the big score. They never mainstreamed Las Vegas. But the gentlemen's clubs of today are a different story. It's people meeting people, with intimate contact assured. The whole town's a big bar now. The whole town is Third Avenue."

Wynn says he has been amazed by observing the powerful allure of the topless clubs for hotel guests, and in making plans for Wynn Las Vegas he felt an obligation to address the trend.

"I understood that things had changed in this town and that I had to understand it and harness that energy," he says.

So he's putting three nightclubs in his new hotel, "so that no one has to leave the joint. I expect these clubs to do $30-$35 million in business with a 40 percent margin."

Wynn says he was not a bit surprised by the black cloud that moved over the Las Vegas topless scene, with the indictment of Jaguars and Cheetah's owner Mike Galardi in San Diego and his subsequent guilty plea, and the indictments brought against several Clark County commissioners, past and present, alleging improper conduct and accepting illegal payments. .

"There are fringy guys running these topless places, with funny buddies," Wynn says. "The money just got too big for them and they couldn't handle the amount of cash coming in."

While Steve Wynn says he won't be the one to lead the charge for county licensing changes that would allow gentlemen's clubs to be owned and operated by the major hotel-casino companies, he admits that he will be cheering for restrictions to be lifted.

"I'm building a place that is two clicks above Bellagio," he says. "I can't have a snotty attitude and look like I'm grubbing at the same time. It's not for me to get out in front of that movement because I'm going to be managing charisma on a different channel here."

His final comment is telling: "But let me say that everything a man would need will be here in our new hotel."

There are rumors popping up weekly that the sexual heat in Las Vegas is getting amped up even higher. *Hustler* magazine publisher Larry Flynt has announced his intention of getting into the topless nightclub industry in Las Vegas, and former Beverly Hills madam Heidi Fleiss has told interviewers that she's considering opening a brothel in Pahrump, just an hour away. I've been told that some of the most expensive homes in Las Vegas, gated-community palaces costing five to 10 million dollars and up, are regularly rented out to adult film producers as settings for XXX-rated films. The payoff is that the homeowner gets to watch the proceedings and participate in any off-camera frivolity.

In the two years I spent researching and writing *Skin City*, rarely a day went by that someone didn't share with me another story dripping with sex that would be "perfect" for my book. I always listen carefully, and wonder whether the wealth of material and anecdotes won't become fodder for a second book. But then another voice tells me that this book alone is enough to consign me to a long stint in purgatory, and if I delve deeper into depravity I'm assured a front-row seat in hell.

As someone who has lived nearly his entire adult life in Las Vegas, and doesn't plan on leaving until I'm thrown out, there's yet another part of me that worries whether this runaway train of sexual permissiveness in Las Vegas, the one that promises that all dark secrets will be kept, and that what happens here stays here, will eventually flatten the village. Sexual freedom behind closed doors, with consenting adults, offers an allure in Las Vegas that will not and should not ever go away. It's woven into the very fabric of the city. But I feel we're walking on a razor's edge in 2004. What will large corporations think about continuing to book conventions here, if half their executives return home sharing tawdry after-hours tales at the water cooler about how they got the wax blown out of their ears in Las Vegas? And now that Wall Street has greatly enhanced its focus on the behavior and morality — or lack thereof — of corporate executives, can it be even remotely possible to license lap dancing in hotels operated by publicly traded companies?

Surely there are blue bloods among our citizenry who are not happy about the direction this community is headed. But no one should be shocked. As a smart friend of mine once said, "There has to be a place in America like Las Vegas where people can do anything their heart desires . . . or at least think they can do anything. Why else do you suppose they put it in the middle of a desert?"—**J.S.**